Camper's Guide to
OUTDOOR COOKING
Tips, Techniques, and Delicious Eats

John G. Ragsdale

Gulf Publishing Company
Book Division
Houston, Texas

Camper's Guide to
OUTDOOR COOKING
Tips, Techniques, and Delicious Eats

Library of Congress Cataloging-in-Publication Data

Ragsdale, John G.
  Outdoor cooking.

  Includes index.
    1. Outdoor cookery. I. Bell, W. I. II. Title.
TX823.R244 1989   641.5'78   88-34817
ISBN 0-87201-626-9

Interior photographs by W. I. Bell
Cover photo © Tom Bean, The Stock Market

Contents

Acknowledgment

I want to thank the many people who have helped in the material for the book—

My wife DeDe for vital review of the recipes and resulting dishes,

My children for support of ideas and recipes,

Neighbors, campers, cooks, and all friends who provided examples for the material.

Preface

The outdoors have provided me with substantial evidence of God's detailed planning and meshing of the continuous progression of life. We have the seasons from the bounding renewal of spring, through the colors of fall, and then the suspended sparkle of winter. I have had the pleasures of hiking on woodland, valley and mountain trails. I have canoed in streams, rivers, and lakes. I have observed wildlife movement and communities, experienced weather varieties, and shared many camping experiences with others.

One of the pleasures of camping is to have a warm, tasty meal. Regardless of the size of your group, such a treat requires proper planning, suitable tools, and appropriate skills. This book has been assembled and written to provide basic information for planning and cooking in camp for small groups of two or three campers to larger groups of eight to ten. The recipes generally are in amounts of food for either four or eight campers, so you may need to adjust the ingredients to suit your group. These recipes can be prepared in your backyard or in a distant wilderness.

I hope the sharing of this information helps you plan your meals, increases your cooking skills, supports you in your cooking occasions, and provides you pleasure in outdoor activities.

John G. Ragsdale
El Dorado, Arkansas

1
Fires

The cheerful glow of a pleasant campfire is highly appealing to most people. It can be a visual, warming, or symbolic center to attract all ages. It can vary from a controlled, intimate fireplace to a huge center stage for a massive crowd. This guide focuses on campfires, fireplaces, and camp stoves as cooking sites/social centers for groups of six to ten persons, and includes fuel gathering and meal preparation.

WOOD

Unless you're using a gas camp stove, you'll need to support ignition of a fire with tinder. Tinder is a dry, easily ignitable material that will begin the flame for our fire. Natural materials may include birch bark from a dead tree, shredded cedar bark, small dead limbs from evergreen trunks or limbs, or the rich-pine or starter-pine heavy with rosin. Once you find the available material you prefer, you probably will want to store some of it in your camping supplies for future use. This tinder can be split and carried in weatherproof containers.

You can also prepare some more advanced material such as paraffin-soaked material to help in your fire starting. I find that a good method is to roll one-inch wide pieces of corrugated cardboard into small cylinders, tie each cardboard cylinder with string, and dip it in some melted paraffin. You may also want to place several wooden matches into a bundle, tie them with string, and dip the bundle in melted paraffin (Figure 1-1). For safety, you should melt the paraffin in a small container that is placed in water in a larger pan over a small

Figure 1-1. Fire starters of corrugated cardboard and matches, dipped in paraffin.

fire. This double-boiler arrangement will allow the paraffin to melt with indirect heat from your stove or fire.

Some people have poured paraffin in cardboard egg cartons; this allows you to later break off a starter section when needed. A further refinement that increases the effectiveness of the starter is to place cedar or pine shavings in the egg carton, and then pour the paraffin over the shavings. Of course, there are treated fiber materials on the market that provide a flammable starter for your kindling, and there are several solid fuel starters available that can directly ignite your wood without using tinder.

Kindling is the small, burnable material that will advance your flaming tinder to a developing fire. This kindling should be small sticks, limbs, or split wood. An ample supply of this should be on hand so that no delay will fall on your growing fire.

Often, you can break small dead limbs from lower limbs of trees, and you can usually find many small limb sections on the ground. If small limbs suitable for kindling are higher in a tree, toss a rope over the desired limb, grasp the rope ends, and pull. If the small limb is dead and dry, it will usually break off. If the limb fails to break relatively easily, it may lack the dry conditions that you would want for your fire use.

If you have split some wood into small strips, these can suffice for the kindling and development of the fire. A few pieces of rich pine, oak, or your choice of material will provide the heat source to continue the fire.

After the fire is well established, you are ready to add the larger fuel items to the fire. This fuel will be your basic fire support. As the fire grows, you can add larger pieces of fuel.

Most wood will burn easier if it is split into smaller pieces that expose more wood surface to the flame. Splitting damp wood will also expose the dry inner wood. Well split wood is the fire keeper's delight.

Table 1-1 shows the qualities of some kinds of wood fuel. You may be limited to local natural material and therefore must prepare the best fire that those conditions allow.

Table 1-1
Firewood Quality

Wood	Kindling	Heat Value
Hardwoods		
Hickory	Medium	Medium
Oak	Good	High
Beech	Medium	High
Birch	Good	High
Maple	Medium	High
Ash	Medium	Medium
Gum	Poor	Low
Willow	Poor	Low
Cottonwood	Poor	Low
Aspen	Poor	Low
Softwoods		
Pine	Good	High
Cedar	Good	High
Fir	Medium	Medium
Spruce	Good	Medium

If you are preparing a fire to boil liquids, you can choose a soft wood that will give you a flame and rapid burning. This type of flame can also serve a reflector oven.

However, if you are cooking food in a skillet, sauce pan, or Dutch oven, you will need coals rather than a flaming fire. This type of fire will best be obtained by using hardwood fuel that has burned to the stage where the whole fuel piece is a mass of coals.

FIRE BUILDING

Choose the size of your fire to fit your cooking needs. Prepare an adequate but not excessive fire for all your cooking. This will limit your firewood requirements and damage to the fire site area.

Choose your fire location for safe usage. Clear the ground surface of burnable material and be certain no adjacent or overhanging vegetation will be ignited or damaged. If the ground is wet, you may need to provide a cover of rocks or non-burnable material for a fire base. Care for the natural area by responsible fire control.

A fire needs three ingredients to burn—heat, air, and fuel. You provide the heat with the initial ignition or with the coals and flames

Figure 1-2. A supply of kindling and fuel wood.

Figure 1-3. Wood supply covered with a rain tarp.

from the existing fire. You provide air by properly placing burnable material on the fire. Fuel comes from the wood you have gathered, split, and kept dry (Figure 1-2).

Carry some plastic sheeting or a tarp to cover stored firewood. This will protect your valuable fuel from rain (Figure 1-3).

To lay your fire, use some tinder at the base or in the middle of your fire lay. Then follow with some of the smallest kindling to provide the material that will ignite from the tinder flame.

One simple fire lay is the lean-to method. Use a rock, brick, log, or diagonal stick to support the top of the kindling when the base of the kindling is on the ground. This will allow air to reach the burnable kindling (Figure 1-4).

A tepee style method can also serve. The kindling can be placed in a tepee conical shape to allow placement of tinder and ignition. The tops of the kindling will be commonly supported and the base of the kindling will be on the ground. Air will be able to reach the burnable kindling (Figure 1-5).

After the tinder is ignited and the kindling begins to flame, add more kindling or some of your smaller fuel pieces. As the fire grows, add more fuel, slowly using larger and larger pieces. Remember, start small fires and add to them.

To aid some reluctant fires, you may want to fan the fire to force air to the flame. Do this gently to keep from extinguishing the flame.

Figure 1-4. A lean-to fire lay.

Figure 1-5. A tepee fire lay.

A slow, steady fanning may salvage the stubborn fire starting. Some fire builders have used a blower to help. This is often a flexible rubber or plastic hose connected to a metal tube that will be nearest the fire. With good kindling, this is usually not necessary.

Except for boiling liquids, cooking should be done with mature coals. These can best be arranged by starting and enlarging the fire at one point and removing sufficient coals to another point for actual cooking. New fuel can be added to the starting fire and become the second batch of coals. It usually is better to have one fire tender to keep the fire and coals sequence in order, thus allowing the cook to concentrate on the cooking.

CHARCOAL

Coals from a good hardwood-fueled fire provide the ideal wood-fired cooking condition. But, many times you will not enjoy this condition because of wood supply or a regulation in force at your cooking area.

A likely substitute for the wood coals is charcoal, a commercially prepared wood product. The lump charcoal must be well ignited and often burns rather quickly.

Charcoal briquets are a good substitute for the wood coals. These processed wood products have been partially charred, blended, and formed into the standard square pillow shape. Briquets burn evenly and will continue to burn until totally consumed.

Ignition of the briquets can be done in an open wood fire, then removed for use. If no fire is available, there are several methods to use for ignition.

A dependable method can be the use of an electric fire starter coil, if electricity is available (Figure 1–6). This usually is a one-loop electric coil with an insulated handle. Place the electric starter coil in a pile of briquets in the fire site, or place the coil in a starter bucket. I find that eight to ten minutes is ample time for the coil to ignite some portion of the briquets. Remove the coil and place it in a safe place to cool. Once the coals are partially ignited, it will take about 10 to 15 minutes to fully ignite the whole bucket of briquets.

One commercial starter bucket I have used is the Auto Fire® can, produced by the Auto Fire® Corporation. This bucket has adequate air openings on the bottom, and a tray to support the briquets about

Figure 1-6. Charcoal briquets ignited with an electric starter.

one-third of the distance from the bottom. The lower one-third of the bucket is for ignition using loosely crushed sheets of newspaper. If the first newspaper doesn't ignite the briquets, a second "edition" of newspaper usually will succeed.

With a starter bucket, coals can be well ignited and then removed with long- handled tongs or a shovel. After some of the briquets have been removed, new briquets can be placed in the bucket for ignition from the existing hot briquets. If you are using coals for several cooking requirements, you can remove ignited briquets and add new ones continuously. I have done this over a couple of hours when multiple coals were needed.

You can easily make a starter bucket by punching air holes in the lowest part of a one-gallon can (Figure 1-7). Other holes can be placed in the bottom of the can, if you can support the can on rocks or metal tent pegs (Figure 1-8). A shaped piece of hardware cloth or fence wire

Figure 1-7. Charcoal briquets ignited in a gallon can supported on bricks.

Figure 1-8. A one-gallon-can charcoal bucket on metal tent pegs.

placed in the lower portion of the can will allow the charcoal to be supported and not compress the newspaper igniter. The newspaper should be placed in the bottom of the can, below the wire. The paper may be ignited through the holes in the bottom of the can.

I have ignited the charcoal in these buckets using a solid fuel, but I prefer the electric igniter or, secondly, the newspaper. Newspaper and a starter bucket are a great help for igniting your briquets. Several buckets may be used if your coal requirements are larger.

I prefer not to use liquid charcoal starter fuel because of safety and odor. The flammable fuel and the open fire are two burnable items too near in the cooking area. The fuel odor may affect any item placed on a grill in the smoke area.

Timing must be considered in using coals. The coals must be prepared early enough to be ready at the cooking time. Generally, ignite your charcoal about 30 minutes before you need to use it. Coals once ignited will continue to be consumed, so replacement coals need to be considered.

Briquets should not have cooking utensils placed directly on them. The air to the charcoal will be restricted and briquets may crumble from the weight. If the briquets are used long enough, a total covering of gray ash will develop over the whole briquet. Gently tap the briquet with tongs and the ash usually will fall away. The freshened charcoal will have a new air exposure.

FIRE TYPES

I generally classify camp cooking fires as one-point or two-point fires. *One-point fires* have a single fire site and any cooking is done in this spot. *Two-point fires* begin at a single starting and burning point, and the fire is extended to a nearby place for cooking.

One-point fires are begun and remain at the starting site. Fuel is added and all cooking is done in the one cooking area. Often, this type of fire type is used for boiling a liquid or cooking only a one-pot item. This fire type can be one in which wrapped items or foil packs can be placed on or in the coals.

Two-point fires are those where the fire is started and fuel is added at the initial site, as above. However, this site is used to continue to burn fuel and provide coals which are removed to an adjacent area.

Figure 1-9. Rocks set to serve as a key-hole fire.

Figure 1-10. A key-hole fire site.

The key-hole fire is an excellent two-point fire (Figures 1-9 and 1-10). The main fire is maintained in a primary site, and coals are removed for cooking in an extended key slot. If the local conditions permit, I like a circular rock walled fire site with a straight key slot

Figure 1-11. Metal grate for support of utensils.

Figure 1-12. A hunter fire of two parallel logs.

of rock sides. The main fire can be continued in the larger circular rock ring to provide coals. Mature coals can be moved to the key slot where cooking can proceed with the ready coals. If rocks are not available, pieces of logs can be used to confine the main fire, and parallel smaller logs can be arranged to confine the coals and provide a cooking area. Metal grates over the cooking rocks or logs give you good support and control of your utensils (Figure 1-11).

A satellite two-point arrangement has the main fire in the fire ring and coals are removed to separate nearby areas. A large main fire can support multiple cooking stations for varied cooking requirements.

The hunter fire is usually defined as a fire between two parallel logs or two parallel rows of evenly sized rocks. This excellent style can serve as a two-point fire with the main fire at one end of the hunter fire and coals raked to the other end for the controlled cooking (Figure 1-12).

2
Stoves

WOOD STOVES

The earlier camp stoves were wood fueled. For a long-term camp, a cast iron or metal stove served well. The simplest style would be a small firebox with a flat top for cooking utensils. This elemental style can be expanded and adapted, for example, by adding an oven.

The size and weight of this type of stove limits its uses in camping. Many individual campers have fashioned wood-fueled stoves from steel drums or cans. For mobile camping or lightweight camping it is not practical.

Using wood for fuel requires timing and draft control. You must begin a fire in time to have it ready to meet your cooking schedule. Draft control on the stove will help regulate the fire burning and heating.

CHARCOAL STOVES

Earlier I mentioned the Auto Fire® starter bucket for igniting charcoal. After coals are ignited, this container can be used as a small stove. A detachable handle is included with the bucket and can be inserted in side holes and used as a bail for moving the bucket.

The handle is also designed with notches in the sides to allow the handle to serve as a support for a cooking pan (Figure 2-1). Placing a pan on this support keeps the pan from closing the top of the container and limiting the fire (Figure 2-2). The handle as placed across the top of the container also gives additional support for your cooking pan. Since the starter bucket base diameter is smaller than the height,

Figure 2-1. Auto Fire® starter bucket with the handle across the top for pan support.

Figure 2-2. Auto Fire® bucket serving as a charcoal stove.

be careful to adequately balance the cooking pan on the stove top. The Auto Fire weighs a few ounces and is easily stored and transported.

Another well designed charcoal stove is the Zalamander stove by the ZZ Corporation (Figure 2-3). This metal double-walled stove has a draft control door, pan support brackets, extended legs, and wire cable handles. Charcoal can be ignited in the stove and a cooking container can be placed on the top of the stove. Fuel is usually charcoal briquets or wood twigs available at your site. The stove weighs about three pounds and is easily transported. Charcoal can be ignited by an electric starter or a solid-fuel starter in the base of the stove.

There are other charcoal stoves or cookers available. One popular type is the cement-lined, metal bucket. Some of these cookers also have an air damper to provide some draft control. A container for cooking is supported on a rack at the top of the stove.

Figure 2-3. A Zalamander charcoal stove.

CAMP GASOLINE

A widely used camp stove is the camp gasoline fueled type. This fuel is a basic gasoline with few additives and moisture free. The fuel is readily available at camping stores, some grocery stores, and hardware stores.

Because of the highly flammable nature of the gasoline, it should be handled carefully. It should only be carried in metal containers, not in any glass or breakable containers. It should be stored in a place safe from spillage or child tampering. Storage out of high temperatures is also advisable.

Many stoves for this fuel are designed with one, two, or three burners. The one burner is light and can serve as a basic cooking heat or supplemental cooking unit.

The two-burner stove top is probably the most popular among campers. This size can provide cooking for two containers or one larger container, and should serve most small groups. The three-burner stove top gives more space and use.

The weight and size of the multiple-burner stove should be evaluated for your camping needs. Two smaller stoves probably would cost more, but would provide more flexibility when cooking your meals.

If you have a camp gasoline lantern, the same fuel for your camp stove will provide an advantage.

An old stove I have used for many years is a Coleman Model 442-A two-burner stove top with wind shields. This unit has a non-rusting, aluminum case, and the whole stove folds into a small suitcase size for storage. It is a family stand-by (Figure 2-4).

LIQUEFIED PETROLEUM

The availability and storage of liquefied petroleum gases for stove fuel have provided wide choices to camp cooks. The fuel, usually propane or butane, is clean-burning and convenient to obtain and use.

Propane is available in most communities. With a fuel container of from 4- to 15-pound sizes, you can provide many hours of fuel usage (Figure 2-5). For your comfort, you might wish to have two fuel containers so one can be carried for refill while a second one is put into

Figure 2-4. A Coleman Model 442-A two-burner stove that uses camp gasoline.

service. A proper valve regulator and pressure hose can be connected directly to your cooking stove.

Some stoves are improved with a diaphragm type fuel valve that helps to provide steady performance at high altitudes or low temperatures. You may find this desirable in your camping conditions.

In addition to the refillable bulk fuel containers, there are smaller, single-use containers available. These single time use containers of propane or butane provide light weight, short term, small stove use. These containers also support lanterns and heaters for your camping.

MULTI-FUEL STOVES

Some stoves are designed to be used with several fuels. The cost may be higher, but if your camping conditions might need these choices, it would be helpful.

Figure 2-5. A Primus Model 4600 two-burner stove that uses propane fuel from a small tank.

Figure 2-6. The MSR X-GK multi-fuel stove.

One such stove is the MSR X-GK which will burn gasoline, kerosene, solvent or diesel oil (Figure 2-6). This stove is designed for tough use.

Figure 2-7. A Coleman Peak 1 Model 550 multi-fuel stove.

The Peak 1 stoves by Coleman have been a boon to backpackers (Figure 2-7). Now the Peak 1 Model 550 has been developed to burn multiple fuels and provide simpler operation.

HOT PLATES

If gas is available, the table top or hot plate stove can be used. These are available in one-, two- or three-burner stoves. Beyond the basic unit are ones with wind screens or table level bases. These can be a valuable long-term camping cooking support.

GELLED FUEL

A basic stove is the one using a gelled fuel. This type is usually a one burner, low BTU unit but does provide a ready heating source. The fuel is usually canned and ready to light when the top is removed.

Conversely, replacing the lid stops the burning, and the fuel can lid retains the fuel for the next usage.

A well known brand is Sterno, and these stoves are often found at complete camping supply stores. The fuel is widely distributed.

BACKPACKING STOVES

The popularity of backpacking has created a demand for lightweight, convenient stoves. Many stoves are available to serve the demands of campers. Fuel can be gasoline, kerosene, propane, or butane, usually. The gasoline will require pumping of a pressurized tank, but it is a readily available fuel that can be carried in sealed containers, and it's cheaper than other fuels.

I have a Coleman Peak 1 Model 400 and find it serves as an excellent lightweight, compact stove. Supporting legs fold out for use and fold away for carrying. After pressure pumping, the stove usually lights easily. A wind screen is provided by the burner support top (Figure 2-8).

Figure 2-8. The Coleman Peak 1 Model 400 camp gasoline stove.

Propane and butane are available in pressurized cartridges and ready to connect to some stoves. Some are "puncture connected" directly to the tank by a hose or tube. The unit heating cost is probably higher, but the convenience is also greater.

Figure 2-9. The GAZ Bleuet Model 206 stove with a small propane tank.

I also have a Bleuet Model 206, which uses butane cartridges, and I find this to be a convenient, heating stove (Figure 2-9). Once the cartridge is punctured and in use, the stove is ready to use with only turning the fuel valve. Since I am not always certain of the previous amount of fuel usage and therefore fuel remaining, I generally carry a new cartridge for the camping trip. No more fuel is a shocking discovery.

Figure 2-10. The Coleman Model 5438-700, a handy one-burner propane stove.

The Coleman model 5438-700 stove is an excellent camp cooking help (Figure 2-10). It is served by a small propane tank that can be removed when not in use. It is a ready heating source as a one burner stove. The wind shield also serves as a support ring for your cooking vessel.

3
Ovens and Smokers

DUTCH OVENS

These cooking vessels may have acquired the name from a source in the early European manufacturing facilities. They were in use in the early years of our country and were a tool for hearth cooking in the home or a reliable campfire utensil for the traveling pioneers.

Usually, the Dutch oven is a round metal pan with a tight fitting lid, long made of cast iron but in recent years also of cast aluminum. The base of the oven has three legs that allow coals to be placed under the oven for basic heat. The lid has a rim on the outer edge to provide retention of coals in the top (Figure 3-1). A fixed handle on the top of the lid provides for lifting the lid. A hinged bail on the edge of the main oven body allows picking up of the whole oven body and lid.

Seasoning a cast iron Dutch oven is very important. This can be done by first cleaning the new oven in hot sudsy water to remove any factory coating on the metal. Then rub a coating of cooking oil on the oven and heat it for an hour or two with low heat. This heating can be in your home oven or with coals from the campfire. After the heating remove the oven, allow it to cool, and make certain that a light coating of oil covers the whole metal surface. This oil coating protects the metal from rusting.

For an aluminum oven (Figure 3-2), wash and dry it. The oven can be oiled for cooking, but I usually wipe it dry for storage before the next use. Rust prevention is not necessary for the aluminum, and for long storage oil may become rancid.

Clean your oven after each use. When a rather dry food item has been cooked, you may be able to wipe the oven clean with a damp

Figure 3-1. A 12-inch cast iron Dutch oven.

Figure 3-2. A 12-inch cast aluminum Dutch oven.

cloth or paper towel. If a messy item was cooked, place some water in the oven and heat the water to boiling, remove the oven from the fire and scrub food particles with a *soft plastic scrubber;* dump the water and food particles. Place a second water wash in the oven and place it on the fire to boil the water. After boiling, remove the oven, scrub the oven with a clean scrubber, dump the water, and let the oven and lid dry. After the oven and lid are dry, rub a light coat of cooking oil on the inner oven surfaces.

For aluminum ovens, clean the oven and lid similarly, but leave the oven dry and not oiled. Since the oven does not need the oil to prevent rusting, it can be stored dry.

The Dutch oven is the one cooking container I would choose first for my outdoor cooking. It can provide a wide variety of camp meals for a small group. The ovens usually are made in sizes from 8 to 16 inches in diameter, with the 12-inch size more widely distributed. This size can generally cook an item to serve 6 to 8 people.

The cast iron ovens are almost three times as heavy and susceptible to rust if unprotected. However, the metal is sturdy, provides a steady heat, and is most satisfactory. The cast aluminum ones are lighter and not susceptible to rusting. They may require a little more care to have adequate coals and heat retention. I have heard reports of aluminum ovens being damaged or warped from over heating, but I have had no such experience.

To use the oven during cooking, there is a bail connected to two sides of the oven and this allows you to lift the whole oven and lid. Usually the bail folds down around the side of the oven if folded in one direction, or to a partially elevated position if folded in the opposite direction. The bail will allow you to lift the oven to inspect or add to the coals under the bottom of the oven or to rotate the oven if heating is uneven.

A fixed handle is on the lid. This allows you to pick up the lid during cooking to inspect or tend to the food. I usually use hot pot tongs or wire lifter for this lid removal. The wire lifter is constructed of 12- or 14-gauge wire about 24 inches long and bent double, allowing a space of about 2 inches between the two parallel sides of the wire. Next, bend a small hook on the bottom inch of each cut end of the wire (Figure 3-3). This gives you a double length of wire to hook under the lid handle, and the 2-inch space allows a place to put a finger or

Figure 3-3. Removing the Dutch oven lid with a wire lifter.

two to assure good control in lifting the lid. Many steel lifter bars have been constructed by individuals who prefer the use of a permanent tool. I often use a steel lid lifter.

Be certain your lid is placed tightly on the oven to allow minimum steam to escape from the oven. A small amount of steam will be forced past the edge of the lid during normal cooking. Because of the excellent expansion property of aluminum, I find I must be certain the lid is fully in place each time it must be lifted and replaced.

Food may be placed directly in the oven or placed in a pan in the oven. I prepare food both ways, depending on the size of the item to be cooked or the need for containment in the oven.

If you are cooking a large roast, a stew or soup, a cobbler with a crusting top, some biscuits that will be browned, or some liquid-steamed vegetables, cook the food directly in the oven. There are few camping dishes better looking than when the Dutch oven lid is removed to reveal a well cooked, simmering, attractive meal.

If you need to cook more than one small container of food, you may want to place separate containers in the oven. I have used oven proof containers or small metal pans for this. Sometimes you may want to construct aluminum foil containers for your separate food items.

If you have a cake or pie that needs to be removed to another area for cutting or serving, you may wish to place the food in a pan in the oven. I usually place a couple of tent pins or nails in the bottom of the oven to support the pan, so heated oven air may circulate all around the pan (Figure 3-4). This also gives you some protection from over heating, if you allowed the underneath coals to become too intense.

Another set of containers I like to use are aluminum muffin cups—gelatin dessert molds or aluminum foil cups (Figure 3-5). I usually

Figure 3-4. Two metal tent pegs in the bottom of the oven to support a baking pan.

Figure 3-5. Muffins in aluminum foil cups cooking in the Dutch oven.

place cup cake papers in the muffin cups to allow easy food removal and reduce washing of the muffin cups.

The versatile Dutch oven can be used without the lid to pan fry, broil, or deep fry foods. The preferable use of the oven is to bake, and any item that can be baked in your kitchen oven can be baked in the Dutch oven, except for size restriction.

Coals are used under the oven and on top of the oven. Generally, for preparing stews, soups or items with large liquid content, you place about two-thirds of the coals underneath the oven and one-third on the top. For baking, you will want to place about one-third of the coals under the oven and two-thirds of the coals on top. With charcoal briquets I usually place six or seven under the 12–inch oven and twelve to fifteen on top (Figures 3-6 and 3-7). As your briquets age and deplete, you will want to add new briquets for long-cooking items. If

Figure 3-6. A Dutch oven lid with coals, supported by two bricks. Even distribution of coals provides even heat.

the ground is damp, you may want to place a piece of foil on the ground to protect your briquets and get maximum heating.

The lid can be inverted and become a useable griddle (Figure 3-8). I usually place three metal tent pegs vertically in the ground to provide a support for the lid. Available rocks or bricks can be used for support of the lid. The slight curvature of the lid is not a great condition to overcome.

PIE PAN OVEN

Another idea for Dutch oven cooks is to construct and use a pie pan oven. This oven is composed of three pie pans—the bottom one in the regular position for containing the food to be cooked; the middle one inverted over the first pan as a lid for the oven; and the top pan in regular position to hold the top coals (Figure 3-9).

Figure 3-7. A coffee cake cooking in a pan in the Dutch oven.

Figure 3-8. The Dutch oven lid inverted for use as a griddle, supported by metal tent pegs.

Figure 3-9. A pie pan oven made from three heavy aluminum pie pans.

The middle pan and the top pan must be bolted together so that when you lift the upper pan of coals, you will also lift the middle pan lid. This allows removal of the top section with one hand when you want to inspect or remove the food in the oven. These two pans can be bolted with one bolt and wing nut placed in a hole made in the center of both pans. A more secure method is to use two bolts and nuts in two holes about 3 to 4 inches apart in the central portion of both pans. Two bolts and nuts also give you a safety factor. In case you lose one nut or bolt, you will have one set to use until a replacement can be secured.

When cooking, these holes will be used to join the middle and upper pans as one piece; when stored, the bolt or bolts can be removed, the two pans turned to nest together, and the bolt or bolts replaced in the holes to keep pans, bolts, and nuts together in a more compact space. The third pan can also then be nested with the other two for storage.

For best results, use heavy gauge, 9-inch aluminum pie pans. Lightweight, alloy pans rust, warp, or conduct heat too poorly to use. Use bolts and wing nuts of a material that will not melt or shed a coating when heated. I use brass ones and have had good results. I have also seen some steel ones that were satisfactory.

Your bottom pan must be supported a short distance above the ground so that coals can be placed under the oven. I have used rocks, but my preference is to use three metal tent stakes equally spaced about two-thirds of the distance from the center of the oven (Figure 3-9). These stakes can be lowered or raised to provide the correct distance above your coals, probably about two inches.

Since aluminum is such a good reflector of heat, I have tried to retain more heat in the oven by painting all surfaces, except the two inside food surfaces, with black boiler paint. I have cooked in identical ovens with and without the black paint coating, and it seems that there is an improvement with the paint. I cannot provide scientific proof, but any small assistance is help in your favor.

A pie pan oven is excellent for backpacking or a canoeing trip when you need minimum space and weight requirements. It also is a good supplemental oven on any trip for baking biscuits or cornbread when another portion of your meal is cooking in your regular Dutch oven. My aluminum pie pan oven and aluminum hot pot tongs are standard packing items.

You may even want to improvise an oven from two heavy skillets in your cooking site. Place the food in the bottom skillet and invert a second skillet for the lid and top-coals support. The bottom skillet can be placed on some coals and other coals placed on the inverted skillet. Care should be taken that coals do not fall from the top skillet into the lower skillet where your food is. You may overcome some of this risk by placing a slightly larger skillet on top, allowing it to lap over the bottom skillet. This arrangement is not as satisfactory as a regular oven, but can be a help.

REFLECTOR OVEN

For times when light weight is critical, you may want to carry and use a reflector oven. The oven can be disassembled for transportation and reassembled for use.

Heat for this oven will come from a flaming fire that reflects from the bright inside surfaces of the oven to cook the food. The flaming fire is one of the times you will not want to use only coals. Your fuel

Figure 3-10. A reflector oven with two 9-inch baking pans.

Figure 3-11. A reflector oven with a hinged back for access to the baking pan shelf.

will be some soft, easily flaming wood. The reflected heat will be directed by the diagonal back pieces to above and below the horizontal food support shelf (Figures 3-10 and 3-11).

It is well to have your oven sized to accommodate two pans on the cooking shelf. I have found that two square 9-inch pans are good sizes. These are usually available in hardware and cooking supply stores, and they can accommodate food volume for a group of six to eight people.

The sketch in Figure 3-12 is for an oven that will accommodate two 9-inch pans. The pieces are designed to fit in a flat container for easy storage. The oven is assembled with common nails that can be readily replaced. It is well to protect the reflective back pieces with cardboard shields directly over the reflective surfaces, then store all pieces in a cloth or other material that will not damage the oven pieces.

If you find the food is too close or too far from the fire, you can move the oven to accommodate it. If you find the pan of food is not cooking evenly on all sides, you may want to rotate the pans. You may find it easier to move the oven from the cooking spot, rotate the pans, and return the oven to the previous cooking site.

STOVE TOP OVEN

Another oven is the stove top that fits over the burner on your camp stove. The oven provides a space to contain the heat from the covered burner and has a thermometer on the oven door to allow measurement of the oven heat (Figure 3-13).

A wire rack is in the oven to allow support of your baking container. A square baking pan is an ideal container to fit the oven and allow maximum oven use.

Experience in using the oven and the thermometer will guide you in the burner heat control for the oven. A pan of biscuits or a hot cake will be a reward for carrying and using the oven.

SMOKERS

A smoker is usually the spacious vessel that provides a tray or container for the meat and a heating source to provide cooking and smok-

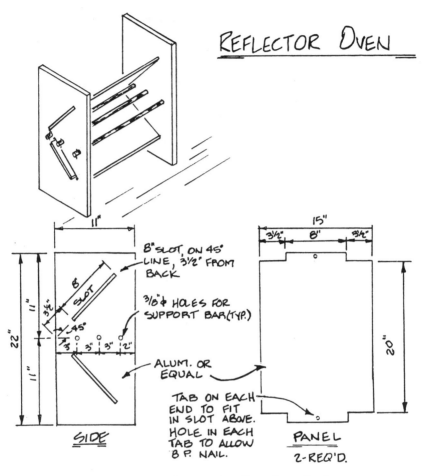

Figure 3-12. A plan for construction of a reflector oven.

ing. There are many commercially prepared smokers or you may want to design and construct your own.

The manufactured smoker may be a horizontal or vertical shape. The horizontal design will usually provide more shelf room for the meat and more space for the heat source, although it also will require more space in your cooking area. The vertical models provide a direct

Figure 3-13. A stove top oven that can bake over a burner.

movement of smoke up from the heat source to the meat and to the top, although shelf space may be less.

The heat source can either be by charcoal or electric coil. The earlier smokers were charcoal fueled, and many subsequent ones have been equipped with electric heating coils.

Charcoal-fueled smokers require that you ignite the charcoal either in a separate igniter or by some starter method in the lower part of the smoker. I usually ignite charcoal in a separate container and place it in the smoker. Additional charcoal can be added when the charcoal volume is partially consumed.

I have used a PK cooker for many years and it has served well. This smoker is of cast aluminum and has adjustable vents in the top and bottom, a divided shelf for the meat, and a lower shelf to support the charcoal. The whole cooker is supported on a wheeled, tubular frame and is very satisfactory (Figure 3-14).

Depending on the type of meat being cooked, we can regulate the air openings on the bottom and the smoke exhaust openings on the top to control the cooking intensity. For short-term cooking, the meat can

Figure 3-14. A typical cast-aluminum, tubular framed, wheeled smoker/cooker with shelves for support of charcoal and food.

be placed on the upper shelf above the charcoal on the lower shelf. For longer term cooking of a brisket, turkey or ham, we place the meat at one end of the upper shelf and a large charcoal supply at the opposite end of the lower shelf (Figure 3-15). Several hours of smoking can provide an excellent meat dish. You should examine the charcoal at intervals of about two hours.

Most smokers are usually constructed of steel or cast aluminum. Some of the steel smokers have an alloy or painted surface for improved performanced.

The smokers must have drafts or air vents to allow for feeding of the charcoal fire and exhaust of the draft. Electric smokers use the

Figure 3-15. A roast in the rear of the smoker and coals in the front.

electric heat source and by use of a little venting, contain the heat and any smoking within the smoker vessel.

Some smokers are fueled by natural gas or propane. These smokers can be mounted on a permanent base or on a portable stand. The steady fuel source provides a constant, controlled heat. Some models are equipped with a multiple rock supply around or over the burning point and this provides some heat stabilization and a method to allow burning of some of the meat drippings.

Braisers are the open container of charcoal or gas fueled burner cookers. These usually have some draft openings in the bottom section for burning control. Probably there are more of these types of cookers used on patios, in backyards, and campsites than any other manufactured cooker. They are usually less expensive and serve for the simple outdoor cooking. Some models have a lid that further allows the brazier to provide some slower cooking and smoking of the food.

4
Pots, Pans, and Utensils

These are items that I prefer to have available for my outdoor cooking. All of the items would not be carried for every camping trip but would be available for your selected use, depending on your number of meals, number of campers, and transportation space. You may wish to prepare your list to serve your needs.

Dutch oven—This would be one of my regular choices, since it is a most versatile cooking vessel. I have cast iron and aluminum ovens in several sizes.

Removable bottom or spring side pans—This is a pan for baking cakes or breads in the oven. My favorite is a 9-inch round pan with a removable bottom. This allows me to loosen the food from the edge of the pan, remove the food from the bottom, and serve it warm.

Skillets—Probably this is the most widely envisioned and used vessel when outdoor cooking is discussed. My choice is a cast iron or cast aluminum one to provide a more constant heat. I prefer to have 6-inch, 10-inch, and 12-inch sizes for variable use. A lid should be available to allow steaming or simmering of some dishes.

Baking dishes—8- and 9-inch pie pans, small oven-proof dishes and aluminum dessert molds for the Dutch ovens; 9-inch or 8-inch square pans for the reflector oven.

Sauce pans—Select several of these multi-use pans, with lids. I enjoy the heavier stainless or cast aluminum ones. There are available some layered-bottom pans that provide a good constant heat; some models are available with folding or removable handles. Some aluminum camp cooking kits have assorted size pans with lids. Some kits have a removable handle to fit several of the pans.

Kettle—A vessel to provide hot water for cooking and preparation of tea, coffee, or hot chocolate is a necessity. This can be the gallon tin can, an aluminum or enameled kettle. I have a lightweight aluminum one that serves us well. I have used enameled ones, too, although you must use care not to damage the enameled surface.

Griddle—A cast iron or cast aluminum griddle is welcome for hot cakes or grilled foods.

Grill—Let's include here a grill for placing over your cooking fire or coals. The grill can be a piece of expanded metal that can be placed on rock or log supports. Some manufactured grills have folding legs, and these are good. If food is to be placed directly on the grill, be sure that no plating or coating of the metal would contaminate the food.

If electricity is available, you may want to include some electric skillets, kettles or grills to use in your cooking. Many commercial camp sites have electrical connections available.

UTENSILS

For tending the fire, coals, and the vessels for cooking, I keep these items:

- Fire starters—wax and solid fuel
- Electric charcoal igniter
- Igniter bucket
- Heavy-duty aluminum foil
- Small shovel

- Hot-pot tongs
- Long-handled coal tong
- Wire lid lifter
- Hot-pan holders
- Long-handled spoon
- Short-handled spatula
- Short-handled pancake turner
- Metal tent pins
- Plastic pan scrubbers
- Hot-pot mitts

For food preparation, I keep these items:

Water container
Paper towels
Mixing bowls
Stirring spoons
Measuring spoons
Measuring cups
Can opener
Paring knives
Slicing knives
Biscuit cutter
Dish water boiling bucket
Dish washing pan
Rubber scraper

CHUCK BOX

You may find it convenient to construct a chuck box to provide a storage place for small utensils, seasonings, and foods. The size can vary from a small suitcase size to a multi-compartment trailer. The size and arrangement should be to serve your needs.

A general type chuck box that will serve the usual needs for a family or small group is shown in Figures 4-1 and 4-2, with a sketch of how to make it shown in Figure 4-3. You may want to vary the dimensions to allow storage of particular tools or utensils.

(text continued on page 46)

Figure 4-1. A chuck box which can serve a small group cooking area.

Figure 4-2. Chuck box closed for transportation or storage.

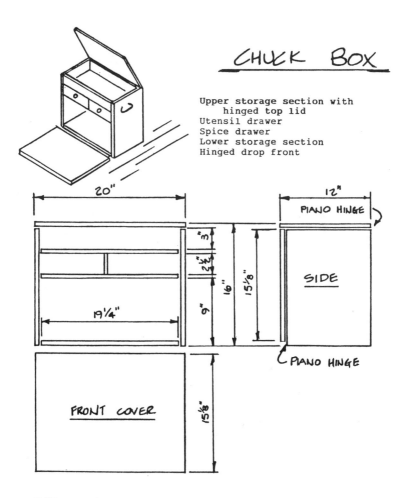

CHUCK BOX

Upper storage section with
    hinged top lid
Utensil drawer
Spice drawer
Lower storage section
Hinged drop front

3/8" exterior plywood
Join pieces with glue and wood screws
Continuous hinge for top lid and drop front
Chest handle on each end
Plastic laminate on top lid and drop front
Front secured with hook and eye
Top lid secured with cabinet latch
Folding brace hinges to support drop front
Metal glide feet on bottom corners
Drawers from 3/8" and 1/4" plywood

Figure 4-3. Plan of a small chuck box.

(text continued from page 43)

The top and the drop front have plastic laminate on them to provide a dough board or food preparation surface. In the small drawer I place seasonings in small cans or plastic containers. The outside of the chuck box can be stained or painted.

5
Trail Cooking

COOKING ON COALS

After you have a bed of coals from your fire, you may want to cook some foods directly on the coals.

One of the easy ways to do this is to use the shell of an orange. First you should cut the orange in half, slicing through the stem end and parallel with the length of the inner sections. This allows the ends of the orange not to be on the bottom of your half of the shell where a small leak could develop. Remove (and eat) the orange sections from the shell and you're ready to use the orange shell as a cooking vessel.

In the orange shell place a ball of ground meat, then place the hull directly on some coals. Cooking of the meat should be about fifteen minutes. You can add some chopped onion, chopped bell peppers, or other seasoning to the ground meat and have a mini meatloaf. Or crack an egg into each half of the orange shell and put it directly on the coals. The egg(s) will take 10 to 12 minutes to cook in the shell (Figure 5-1).

You may choose to use a part of a whole onion for the "cooking pot." Cut the onion in half, slicing across the middle of the onion. Then remove the inner sections, leaving the outer two or three rings still connected. Place ground beef or egg in this holder and put the onion section on some coals. Cooking time will be similar to that in using the orange shells.

You can also place vegetable pieces in the orange shell or onion shell to cook. Also, biscuit dough can be cooked in this manner.

Want to cook some corn on the cob in your coals? First peel back the corn shucks about half way, remove the silk, moisten the corn and

Figure 5-1. Cooking biscuit dough, ground beef, and an egg in orange shells.

replace the shuck. Place the ear of corn on some coals and cook for about 5 minutes; rotate the ear of corn one half of a turn and cook for an additional 5 minutes.

Have you ever baked a potato coated with mud? If clay is available, moisten some of the clay and cover the potato with a coating about 3/8-inch thick. Clay soil is better, but you can use sandy soil if necessary. You should make the sandy mud coating thicker to allow it to adhere to the potato. Puncture the potato with a knife point and wrap with the mud. Place the potato in a bed of coals, cover it, and allow it to cook about an hour. When you remove the potato from the coals, tap the mud layer, which is now fire baked, and the coating should fall off. The potato should be ready to serve.

A more indirect method of cooking is to heat some flat rocks in the fire. If you are in an area that has no natural rocks available, you may want to use bricks. Be certain these rocks or bricks are not too porous or moisture laden, because they might explode when the heat turns the water to steam. After the rocks or bricks are heated, remove them from the fire and use the heated rocks or bricks for a flat cooking surface. Rub some margarine on the surface and place some small meat pieces on it to cook. After a few minutes, turn the meat once and serve when it is cooked.

Did you know you can boil water and cook in a paper cup? This cup should be a plain paper cup, not waxed. Place a cup of water on the ground and put coals or charcoal briquets closely around it, but *not* touching it (Figure 5-2). When the water is heated, it can be used for preparing a hot drink or for soup from an envelope of soup mix. The liquid in the cup and a small space between the cup and coals will allow heating without burning the cup.

Figure 5-2. Boiling water in a paper cup surrounded by charcoal.

Figure 5-3. Corn meal cake cooking on a hoe head.

Try preparing hoe cakes. In past generations when row crops were tended by field workers, the hoe was a common tool. Sometimes on the fire in the hearth of the house or at a fire in the field work area, the hoe blade could serve as a flat cooking area. Some corn meal batter could be placed on the hoe blade, which was placed on or above the coals, and soon the hoe cakes were cooked (Figure 5-3). After cooking on one side, the cakes could be turned to brown on the other side. Some margarine smeared on the hoe blade might prevent sticking. Any flat steel item might be used for the cooking surface.

TIN CAN USES

Tin cans, especially the one-gallon size, are readily available from kitchens in restaurants, cafeterias, schools, and churches. Presently, few recycling programs exist for these cans, so they are usually a trash item. You, too, can use these expendable cans and not have to wash "dishes" afterward. For your outdoor cooking these cans are a good resource once they are washed well for camp usage, which includes:

Mixing—Use cans for a mixing bowl. Mix biscuit dough, pancake batter or cake batter in the can. I sometimes use a green limb for a stirring stick. Select a palatable hardwood limb and shave the bark off, exposing a clean stirring tool. You can discard the stirring stick with the can.

Boiling—Boil water for cooking. Use water for recipes, hot tea, chocolate, or coffee. You may lift the can with hot pot tongs; you may want to punch two holes near the rim, on opposite sides and place a wire bail on the can. A foil cover keeps ashes out of the can.

Soup—Mix and cook your soup or stew in the can. You may want to place an aluminum foil lid on the pan. Serve the food from the can to the plates.

Eggs—Boil water in the can and prepare soft boiled or hard boiled eggs. Remember to prick the large end of the egg with a small knife point to allow pressure equalization, to avoid cracking the egg during boiling.

Cereal—Cook oatmeal, cream of wheat, or grits in the can.

Vegetables—Place margarine in bottom of the can and stir cook some sliced vegetables.

Popcorn—Place margarine and popcorn in the covered can. Agitate the can occasionally during cooking.

Baking—Place biscuits in the can with a foil cover on the can. Place coals under or around the sides of the can (Figure 5-4).

For better results in most cooking in cans, place the cans on a support so the can will not rest directly on the coals. This will help in not mashing or smothering the coals. The support of the can can be by rocks, bricks, metal tent pegs, or a grill across the fire.

You may want to use tin cans for expendable stoves. Cut three flaps half way down from the top of the can; bend the flaps fully into the inner side of the can. Be careful when cutting the can—the edges are *sharp*. Folding the flaps into the can will be safer than leaving the cut flap edges exposed. To provide for smoke to escape from the stove, you should use a beverage can opener and punch two holes in the bottom of the side of the can. Now you can invert the can, coals can

Figure 5-4. Baking in a covered can surrounded by coals.

Figure 5-5. A can stove with coals under the can.

Figure 5-6. Gelled fuel serving as can stove.

be placed under the can and soon a heated stove can be used for limited cooking (Figure 5-5). If the stove top needs to be nearer the coals, bend the support members to a shorter length. You may place the food item directly on the stove (can), such as a meat patty or egg. You may even place a small cooking container on the stove.

Instead of charcoal, you may put a can of gelled heating fuel under the stove. Adjust the height of the flame by a brick or rock under the fuel can (Figure 5-6).

Another can use for many years has been the "buddy burner." This is made by placing some absorbent material in a short can, and then pouring melted paraffin on top. This flammable paraffin can be ignited for a heating source (Figure 5-7).

The can should be the size that holds 8 ounces of sliced pineapple or tuna fish. Cut strips of corrugated cardboard and roll to fit in the can. Next, melt the paraffin in a double boiler arrangement where the larger, outer pan contains the heated water and the smaller pan contains the paraffin for melting. This use of an indirect heating of the paraffin is safer than direct melting of paraffin in a can directly on the fire.

Figure 5-7. "Buddy burners" made from tuna or sliced-pineapple cans provide portable, disposable heat sources.

SUPPORTED/SUSPENDED COOKING METHODS

An old method of cooking meats or some other foods has been the use of a spit or similar tool. The spit is usually a slender steel rod that is inserted through the food and then suspended across the cooking coals by supports under both ends of the spit. I prefer a flat, blade-shaped spit that gives some assistance in firmly grasping the food when the spit is rotated.

Another thing to consider is the cooking of more than one kind of food that requires different amounts of time to cook. You may want to cook the longest time food first and add other items later, so that all are done at finishing time. You can have several spits and place each food item on separate spits, so the different foods can be placed over the fire at different times.

A spit can be made of a green tree limb. Choose a tree that has no tendency to impart a poor taste to the food. A hardwood limb such as hickory or oak will also better resist burning when used over the fire. I usually shave a spit to make the sides flat and the cross section in the shape of a rectangle, to assist in keeping the cooking item from turning when rotated.

Figure 5-8. Biscuit dough cooking on a green limb.

If you are cooking bread on a stick, you will need a different spit. I use a green limb of about 1 to 1¹/₂ inches in diameter. If there are a few branches on the limb, leave slight protrusions on the limb where these branches were. I also usually cut some grooves around the limb. With any protrusions and grooves on the limb, the moist dough will usually cling to the spit (Figure 5-8).

Mix your dough from a biscuit mix or biscuit recipe, roll or pat the dough into strips about 2 inches wide and long enough to fit the length of your cooking portion of the spit. Moisten your spit and wrap your dough in a diagonal strip around the spit, leaving a slight space between wraps of the dough. Press the dough gently so it will cling to the protrusions, grooves or rough places on the spit. I prefer the dough thickness about ¹/₄ to ³/₈ of an inch in thickness.

Place the dough spit over the coals and rotate the spit occasionally to cook the dough evenly. If the bed of coals is even and the dough thickness even, it will usually cook evenly. You should observe the cooking of the dough to raise or lower the spit height to cook the bread completely through the dough thickness before the outside is too brown. Break the bread off in small pieces and serve to the group.

A modification of the spit is the leaning-stick spit. This spit is supported by rocks or logs so the food containing portion of the spit is

Figure 5-9. Water heating can supported by a dingle stick.

over the coals. Usually this spit should be longer to provide a better support base. Care must be taken that the spit is at an angle so the spitted food will cook evenly.

A dingle stick is a limb or metal bar that is supported at one end and the other end left suspended over the fire or coals. The suspended end of the dingle stick can hold the bail of a can or kettle, or a wire that supports food (Figure 5-9). Notches in the dingle stick will provide firm placement of the hanging bail or wire. Moving the hanging wire from one notch to another notch can raise or lower the cooking food above the coals.

Another method of support of food over coals can be the vertical support from a tripod or metal support bar. The string or wire holding the food can be suspended from the tripod or support bar. The string or wire can be lowered or raised to accommodate heat magnitude to cook the food.

Figure 5-10. Meat cooking on a vertical spit of two metal tent pegs wired together.

Additionally, impaled food can be cooked adjacent to coals. Wire, steel bar, or a metal tent peg might be used for a vertical spit to support the food. If the food is cooking more at the bottom than the top, the food can be reversed on the vertical spit (Figure 5-10).

In the use of all of these vertical supported cooking methods, an enhancement can be used. This is the use of a reflective wall near the fire. This reflector can be a flat wall or an L-shaped piece to reflect heat to the cooking item. This reflector can be a firm metal or aluminum foil piece. Either can assist the cooking of the food.

ALUMINUM FOIL

This most popular material has provided a versatile method in outdoor cooking, since the foil is relatively inexpensive, readily available, and easy to use. I prefer to use the heavy-duty foil since this gives a little more assurance in using a container that will not leak through a puncture or creased fold.

Probably the most widely used foil cooking use is the envelope or rectangular folded package. Tear off a piece of foil about three times as long as you want the completed food package to be. Place the food on the foil and fold the foil in half so the food is in between the folded pieces, near the fold (Figures 5-11 and 5-12). (When placing food in the package, I usually add a tablespoon of water to generate steam, if the other food to be prepared is a bit dry.) Then, beginning at the place where the two end edges are, make a fold of about 1/2 inch and firmly press this, sealing the seam. Then fold the seam over two other folds and press down firmly.

Next, go to one edge of the food package, fold a 1/2-inch sealing seam and fold the seam over two additional times. Go to the opposite edge and again make a three-fold seam. This should now seal all edges of the food package and make it ready to place on the cooking fire (Figures 5-13 and 5-14).

Figure 5-11. Aluminum foil and food to be wrapped.

Figure 5-12. First fold of a foil wrap.

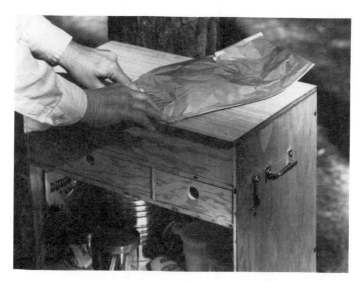

Figure 5-13. Second fold of a foil wrap.

Figure 5-14. Completing the foil wrap with a third side fold.

Figure 5-15. Foil wrapped food on coals.

The food package can now be placed directly on the coals or on a grill over the fire (Figure 5-15). Be careful to make sure the foil is not punctured in handling or cooking. The pressure tight package provides steam for cooking and any leakage in the package will allow the moisture to escape and the food will be burned by the fire heat.

Another use of foil is to form a reflector or wind shield for your cooking vessels. The foil can be wrapped around poles in the ground or around metal grills.

You may also form a pan or container in which food can be cooked. Press some foil around a can or container to make the size and shape container you need. Remove the foil, place the food in the foil, and place the foil in the place where the food will cook. Such food containers can be placed directly on coals, on a grill, in a pan, or oven.

You can also prepare a pan-shaped container for use. Take a forked limb and make a triangular-shaped pan for cooking by wrapping the foil over the forked limb. Be sure to use enough foil to provide sufficient pan depth and wrap enough foil over the limbs to safely hold the cooking food.

Some food items can be wrapped in foil and placed in the coals to cook. Try wrapping potatoes, placing them in a bed of coals for an hour; remember to puncture the potato with a knife blade before wrapping. Wrap an egg and cook on the coals for about 5 to 8 minutes. Wrap an acorn squash half in foil and cook about 20 minutes in the coals; add a spoon of water in the foil wrap to provide steam during cooking. When wrapping the food, twist one end of the foil to form a tail to give you a handle to place the food on the fire.

Try a banana split. Slice one side of a banana from end to end; gently open the banana and place some brown sugar and chocolate chips in the middle of the banana. Wrap this in foil and cook for about 5 minutes. If you prefer, place brown sugar and raisins in the banana.

One use of foil for Dutch ovens is to place a piece of foil, slightly larger than the oven, on the ground under the oven. This will keep ground moisture from chilling your coals or briquets and also give some heat reflection.

BACKPACKING

Reducing weight and conserving space are prime concerns when backpacking, and they certainly apply to cooking on the trail. The extent of your trip can vary from a short hike to several days on the trail. So, pack light. (See Chapter 2, "Stoves," for lightweight backpacking stoves.)

Non-cook lunches will require cooking only morning and evening. The non-cook meal can be carried by individual campers or in a one-meal package by one or two people. Be sure the food is in waterproof bags.

Many freeze-dry foods are available in camping specialty stores and from mail order companies. You can purchase individual food items or you can purchase pre-packed meals for each meal of the day. Some of these items may require cooking for a short time, but many only require hot water, stirring, and a few minutes to be rehydrated. These can provide good meals with minimum preparation time.

Pack your food in plastic bags with sealing ties or zipper-type closures. Individually-packed items can be put in a larger bag to contain the whole meal.

Label the bag to indicate the meal and the day of use. All meals can be prepared in this manner and divided among the campers for weight and bulk distribution.

Drinking and cooking water must be available. Before your trip, check the water supply and plan to carry necessary water between supply points.

You can supplement your freeze-dry food with dry foods from your local grocery stores. These dry or canned items are generally available:

Dry foods: pasta, beans, peas, rice, grits, cornmeal, wheat flour, crackers, fruit, instant soup, nuts, and jerky.

Canned foods: meat, vegetables, fruit, soup.

Other foods: cheese and candy.

CANOEING

For the ease of portage of camping supplies and for a weight control of your loaded canoe, pack minimum, light supplies. This is a matter of experience and opinion on packing many items, but less weight will be beneficial.

Pack your food supplies for each meal in a waterproof plastic bag, labeling the bag with the name of the meal and day for use. These meal supply bags can be further consolidated in another bag labeled for the day of use. These food bags can now be packed with other gear for travel. Protect the bags from punctures or tears so water will not harm the food.

Potable water will be needed for drinking and cooking. If water is not available at cooking sites, it may be necessary to carry water. Carry water in plastic jugs and secure these in the canoe.

6
Meal Planning and Cooking Tips

When preparing menus and food lists for outdoor meals, remember to balance them with the basic food divisions—meats, vegetables, fruits, milk, and cereals—you can plan the items to serve these.

BREAKFAST

Fruits—Raw fruits are easy to carry and can be well used. Try apples quartered, oranges cut in eighths, bananas, grapefruit halved and section sliced, peaches sliced, cherries, cantaloupe peeled and cut in small cubes, melons cut in slices.

Cooked fruits can be apples flavored with sugar and cinnamon, dried fruit soaked overnight and served cool or warmed.

Dried fruit can be served from the container. These can provide a tasty, chewy item.

Canned fruits provide a source for varied servings. Place these in a serving vessel for the group.

Eggs—This standard breakfast item can be prepared several ways. Break the eggs in a bowl, add a few tablespoons of milk or water and scramble the eggs in a skillet. Be sure the other items are cooked and kept warm so that all can be served warm at once.

Boiled eggs can be prepared well. Boil sufficient water to allow all eggs to be covered by the water. Puncture a small hole in the shell in the large end of the egg. Place the eggs in the boiling water, cook about 5 minutes for a soft boiled egg or 15 minutes for a hard boiled egg.

Fried eggs can be cooked in a skillet or on the griddle. Rub the bottom of the vessel with margarine, break the eggs, and place each egg on an open space on the vessel. Cook for a few minutes, turning the egg over for longer cooking, if desired.

Poaching can be done in a skillet using some water about ½ inch deep. Use a fruit jar lid ring or an aluminum foil ring to contain each egg. Lift the egg with a flat lifter after cooking about 5–7 minutes.

Meats—Bacon can be cooked by individual pieces in a skillet, but this is very time consuming. I prefer to place a pound of bacon on a cutting surface and cut all slices in half, then place all of the bacon in the skillet or Dutch oven. One pound can serve four to six persons, so use the amount to serve your group. Stir the bacon occasionally to move the less cooked bacon to the cooking surface, and remove the liquid grease regularly. The meal's bacon should be ready in minimum time.

Sausage can be either the link or bulk type. Place the links or patties in a skillet or open base of the Dutch oven, and turn the meat to cook all sides. Drain excessive grease.

Ham or other sliced meat may be cooked in a skillet or open Dutch oven. If you wish to steam or simmer the meat, you can place a lid on the container. The meat will brown more if cooked with the lid off.

Canned meats are available that require no refrigeration. Most of these meats are already cooked and require only warming for use in your meal.

Cereal—A real favorite is oatmeal. This is usually available in instant, quick, or "a few minutes more" cooking. The instant type is usually in individual packages for mixing with boiling water. This may be good for use in backpacking or when each camper is to carry his or her own personal food.

Other types of oatmeal can require cooking times of from 1– 5 minutes. These will usually be the choice of many campers. Use brown sugar or honey when adding some sweetener to the oatmeal. Add raisins to the oatmeal while it is cooking, if you wish. Give the choice to each camper and provide raisins to be added to individual servings, if desired.

Regular oatmeal can be used, although you must allow for the cooking time of 5–8 minutes. Your time is rewarded by the wholesome flavor, though.

Cracked wheat is a great dish for breakfast. Cook this in a large pan or can and serve with the choice of brown sugar or honey.

Cream of wheat is easily prepared in a large container and can serve your whole group.

Grits can be prepared in a similar way to serve your group. Add margarine and brown sugar as desired.

Breads—Freshly cooked breads can really enhance your breakfast. Bake some biscuits or muffins in your oven and serve with a margarine spread and jelly. Prepare enough so people can have seconds.

Hot cakes require only mixing and cooking on the griddle but are usually a welcome breakfast. Heat some water in a pan and warm your container of syrup; this is a must for great hot cakes. If you are using metal or crockery plates, warm these near the fire, further improving the serving of warm cakes. If you want variety, place a few raisins, chocolate chips, or berries on your griddle, then pour the batter over these. When you flip the hot cakes the added item will be imbedded and show at the then top of each hot cake.

Beverages—Drinks for breakfast can be cold or hot. Juices can be cooled and poured into each serving cup. Individual containers can be provided for each camper to select. For hot drinks, have boiling water to provide for hot tea, hot chocolate, or coffee. Those can be available to each camper by tea bag or individual packets, or a large pot can be prepared for all to use.

LUNCH

Generally, I prefer a non-cook lunch. This reduces your preparation time and also allows your campers to have the option to carry some items with them if they will be away from the main camp at lunch time.

If your campers will be in the campsite at lunch time, you can plan to use foods from the ice box or from previously prepared items, which need not be refrigerated.

Sandwiches are often the fare for lunch. These can be prepared and stored before lunch, can be carried on a trip away from the camp area, or can be prepared at the lunch site. If your regular sandwiches have been prepared from the usual items, try some variety.

Bread is the basic support for your sandwiches, but in addition to your regular bread, try some others such as pumpernickel or rye. Many crackers are available to provide the tasty bread for the meal.

Cheeses are a prime source of filling for the sandwich. Some cheeses need refrigeration, but some do not. "Warm" cheese is often tastier. An abundance of cheeses can serve as the main sandwich ingredient.

Meats can be the focus of lunch or just another layer in your sandwich. Sliced, refrigerated meats, of course, provide an easy meal. With the meats, you may want some of the prepared spreads of mustards, horseradish, or relishes.

Canned meats provide a variety of items for lunch. Some meats can be served from the can. Place salmon or sardines on a serving plate. Take pork or beef from the can, slice and serve. Some small sausages or meat items can be used from the can.

Take some potted meat or tuna from the can, mix with your preferred filler, and serve.

Fruits are a wonderful thing for the meal or for dessert. Fresh seasonal fruits for use could be peaches, pears, apples, or melons.

Dried fruits are usually available year-round and can be carried with no refrigeration. These can be eaten dry or rehydrated before the meal.

Candy bars and wrapped items can be used. These can be served at meals or snack times.

Trail mixes can be used any time. Try using cereals, nuts or fruits singularly or mixed.

Cereals—Try packaged items or rolled oats.

Nuts—Almonds, peanuts or pecans. These can be raw or toasted. They can be salted, sugared, coated or plain.

Fruits—Raisins, dates, dried apples, pears, pineapples, peaches, bananas.

DINNER

This is the time to have a great meal to cap a busy day, when everyone has gathered at the campsite or in the backyard.

A favorite of mine is the one-dish meal. This is a combination of ingredients in the one pot or dish to be served. It can be a stew or soup or combination of items you like.

If you are preparing meats, vegetables, breads, or desserts, your timing will be similar to cooking in a kitchen. Know when the meal is to be served, and plan the cooking to end with the foods ready at the meal time. If you are using a campfire, this means preparing the coals early enough to allow time for cooking.

Meat, usually the main course, can be prepared in a container on your stove or bed of coals, on spits or rotisseries in a cooker, on a grill over the open coals, or on coals in the backyard cooker or smoker.

Soup is a basic outdoor dish that can serve the hungry campers or the group in the backyard. This can be a preliminary meal for early arrivers, or it can be the main dish when accompanied by a hearty vegetable dish and some hot biscuits. Try a bean soup or chowder for the group.

Some instant soups that require only boiling water provide a variety of tastes. These can be good for any meal or on your backpacking menu. Some commercial soup mixes can be prepared readily with a base liquid and only a few minutes for preparation.

Vegetables can be a prime part of your meal. Think of the multitude of potato uses—baked, fried, boiled, or in casseroles. These can be cooked in the coals, in open skillets, in sauce pans, or in dishes in an oven.

Also, consider bean dishes—baked beans, a simmered pan of beans, a casserole, or even beans that can be served cold.

A wonderful variety of other vegetables—squashes, tomatoes, carrots, corn—is available. The vegetable colors of green, white, yellow, and orange contribute to your choices.

Salads can be a good part of your meal, and should usually be prepared before the meal to save time. Go beyond the plain lettuce and tomato serving. Include raw vegetables—cauliflower, broccoli, yellow squash, zucchini, spinach—and seasonings—celery seed, parsley or dill. You can even add yogurt, small cubes of cheese, or cottage cheese.

Try a congealed salad with gelatin and some fruit in it. Use fruit with a desired sauce.

Bread is usually expected at meals, indoors or outdoors. It can be "store-bought" or freshly cooked at the camp fire or stove.

A simple start for fresh hot bread would be biscuits in a Dutch oven or bannock in a skillet. With the use of biscuit mix, you can prepare the dough with use of only water or milk and have a warm treat for the meal. Biscuits with margarine and jelly are usually a welcome part of any meal.

Many bread items call for baking powder or baking soda for ingredients. These can be carried and used for great results.

Go further and try some yeast-raised breads—loaf breads or rolls. These will require more timing before the meal and usually a closed, warm place for rising, but the results can be worth it. First, try a simple white bread and later modify your cooking for mixed flours and varied breads.

You can use the frozen or refrigerated bread doughs from the grocery stores and have a good bread item for your outdoor meals. These can easily be baked in your oven.

Desserts, for many of us, are the real dish we delight in preparing. You can plan a cobbler, cake, pies, or muffins, which can be served warm, or cookies or cooled pudding, which can be prepared ahead. The use of fruits or sauces can enhance a dessert serving.

For snack serving or a backpacking meal, you can use prepared candy packs, canned fruit or your own pre-packed desserts.

DISHWASHING

This is a chore that must be faced, so plan ahead to minimize the problems. The pleasures and support of well prepared, tasty meals make the dishwashing worth it.

★ Heat your dishwashing water during the meal so the water will be ready at the end of the meal.

★ If cooking on an open fire, rub liquid soap, or a paste of powdered soap on the outside of cooking pots and pans. This soap base will keep the flame black from adhering to the containers and will make washing easier.

★ If all dish washing is done by camp fire, it will be best to scrub food from the food dishes in a water rinse, wash the dishes in a hot soapy water, rinse in a hot rinse, and scald dishes in a final rinse.

★ Sanitizers and chemical additions to the hot water rinses may provide additional support in having sanitary dishes and utensils.

★ Drain dishes and air dry. The less wiping with a cloth the less handling and time spent.

★ Of course, paper plates and plastic utensils will eliminate much dish washing, if they are practical.

COOKING TIPS

★ Prepare cracker or cookie crumbs by placing the crackers or cookies in a plastic bag and crumbling them in the bag by hand or rolling pin.

★ To cover some small food pieces with dry seasonings or dry ingredients, place the dry material in a paper sack, add the food pieces and shake them in the sack.

★ Cooked food pieces can be kept warm by placing them in a corrugated cardboard box or a paper bag that has been lined with several layers of newspaper or wrapping paper.

★ Heat plates by placing them near the fire or stove. This will assist in keeping warm food warm. Heat cups with boiling water for a minute or two, discarding the hot water, then put hot drinks in the heated cups.

★ Place a tablespoon of cooking oil in a pan of rice or beans to be cooked so the oil can calm the contents to reduce boiling over.

★ Keep pancake or waffle syrup warm by placing the pitcher or bottle in a larger container of hot water. Remove the bottle lid so pressure will not increase when the bottle is heated.

★ To better contain and remove paper towels, remove only the end of the wrapper of the towel roll, then twist and remove the cardboard core of the roll. This allows removal of each sheet of paper towel from the center while keeping the roll intact and without the outside sheets being loose. Protect the contained roll of towels by keeping the roll in a gallon can or cardboard box.

★ Before your camping or outdoor trip, prepare and package many of the food items in the kitchen for time saving and cleanliness. Chop, cube, or slice the vegetables and seal in plastic bags. Measure and seal in plastic bags dry cake, pancake, or biscuit mix the day before the trip; add fresh or wet ingredients at the cooking site. Carry crumbled toppings in small separate packages. Slice or cube meats, seal in plastic bags and refrigerate.

★ To reduce the water in the bottom of the ice box, place ice in a sealable plastic container. A large-screw, lidded plastic jar is great for this. Water can be placed in clean one-gallon or one-half gallon plastic bottles and frozen in the home freezer. These can later be used in the ice box.

★ Cooking oil can be stored in a screw-lidded plastic jar to avoid use of a breakable bottle. Be certain the lid seals well.

★ Store spices and small food items in small, sealable plastic containers. These can be placed in the chuck box or food storage box. Label each container. Be certain the baking powder and baking soda are fresh and dry.

★ Place fire blackened grills in corrugated boxes or cloth bags for clean handling and storage. These boxes or bags can be constructed from available materials. Larger pots or water heating buckets can be placed in burlap sacks.

★ Before boiling eggs, punch a small hole in the large end of each egg. This allows expansion and may prevent cracking of the egg. A map tack or any needle-type pointed tool is good for puncturing the eggs.

★ Boiled eggs can be peeled easier while the eggs remain warm. Store the peeled eggs in a sealed container to keep them from becoming discolored.

★ If raisins are to be added in some recipes, cover the raisins with water and soak them for several hours to hydrate them for plumpness.

★ Remove eggs from cooler and have them at open temperature before using.

★ Yogurt can be substituted for sour cream in recipes.

★ To bake a cake that needs a tube pan, make a temporary one. Oil baking pan, then place a 2-inch diameter juice or vegetable can in the center of the cake pan, providing a well for heating the center of the cake. The small can should have the top removed, be empty, and be oiled on the outside, which will be surrounded by batter. Use a can with no paint or ink on the can, which might flake off in cooking; or wrap the can in foil, if any paint is on the can. Hold the small can in place when pouring the batter in the baking pan.

★ Check a baking cake for doneness by inserting a straw or tooth-pick to the bottom of the pan. Pull the straw from the cake. Any crumb or batter adhering to the straw indicates the cake is not done; a clean straw indicates the cake is done.

★ Six double graham crackers crushed equals a cup.

Food Substitutes

If you find that you lack some food items, you can often substitute another ingredient to allow you to prepare the food. These are some basic ideas I like to remember:

1 tbsp cornstarch = 2 tbsp flour

1 cup sugar = ¾ cup honey

You may want to slightly reduce any other liquids in your recipe to compensate for this honey liquid volume

1 1-oz square of unsweetened chocolate = 1 tsp margarine plus 3 tbsp cocoa

1 cup milk = ½ cup evaporated milk plus ½ cup water

1 cup milk = ⅓ cup dry milk plus ⅞ cup water

1 cup margarine = 1 cup butter = ⅞ cup cooking oil

Abbreviations

oz = ounce

tsp = teaspoon

tbsp = tablespoon

lb = pound

pkg = package

qt = quart

ml = milliliter

Metric Conversion

1 tsp = 5 ml

1 tbsp = 15 ml

1 cup = 237 ml
1 pint = 471 ml
1 qt = 942 ml
1 oz = 28 grams
1 lb = 454 grams

Measurements
3 teaspoons = 1 tablespoon
4 tablespoons = 1/4 cup = 2 ounces
5 1/3 tablespoons = 1/3 cup
1 cup = 8 ounces = 1/2 pint
2 cups = 16 ounces = 1 pint
4 cups = 1 quart
1/3 cup dry milk plus 7/8 cup water = 1 cup milk
1 1/3 cups dry milk plus 3 3/4 cups water = 4 cups milk = 1 quart
1 stick butter = 1/4 pound = 1/2 cup = 8 tablespoons

Baking Temperatures
When using a reflector oven or a Dutch oven, you will not have a known temperature. A small metal, spring-activated thermometer can be placed in the oven. Some stove top ovens may have a thermometer built in for your use. For your reference these oven temperatures can be used.

	°F	Minutes
Biscuits	450	10–15
Muffins	375–400	15–20
Corn Bread	425	12–15
Yeast Rolls	400	10–12
Pie Crusts	450	10–12
Layer Cake	350–375	20–40
Tube Cake	325–350	30–60
Cookies	350–375	10–15

Definitions
Some folks reading this guide are new to cooking, and others are experienced cooks who have their own ideas about it. So, to make

sure we are all talking the same language, you might want to check over the following definitions:

Bake—Cook with dry heat in an oven.

Beat—Blend thoroughly with a beater, whisk or spoon.

Blanch—Dip into boiling water for a short time, then usually dip into cool water.

Blend—Combine all ingredients thoroughly.

Boil—Cook in water when liquid bubbles well.

Braise—Cook in a small amount of oil or margarine in a pan.

Bread—Dip in a beaten egg mixture and then coat with crumbs or flour.

Broil—Cook meat directly over fire on spit or grill.

Brown—Cook on all sides in an open pan or container in a small amount of oil.

Brush—Spread liquid on top.

Chill—Cool in ice box or refrigerator.

Chop—Cut into small pieces.

Coat—Cover with a thin layer.

Combine—Mix thoroughly.

Cream—Mix all ingredients until creamy.

Cube—Cut into cubes.

Dice—Cut into small cubes.

Dissolve—Heat or stir until a substance goes into solution.

Flake—Break into small pieces.

Fold—Fold one portion of food over with minimum force.

Fry—Cook in cooking oil.

Grate—Move food through small grater openings.

Grill—Cook on grill or grate placed over direct heat of fire.

Knead—Work dough by folding and pushing.

Marinate—Place in seasoned liquid.

Mince—Cut into small pieces.

Mix—Combine ingredients thoroughly.

Pan fry—Cook in a small amount of oil or margarine in a pan.

Par boil—Boil until partially cooked.

Parch—Cook by dry heat.

Peel—Remove skin or outside layer of fruit or vegetable.

Poach—Cook in hot liquid.

Roast—Cook by dry heat in oven.

Saute—Cook in a small amount of oil or margarine in an open pan.

Scallop—Bake food in a sauce.

Simmer—Cook in liquid with small amount of bubbles, usually in a covered container.

Skewer—Place meat or vegetables on metal rods to hold over fire or pan.

Sliver—Slice nuts.

Spit—Metal rod or wooden limb to support food over fire.

Sprinkle—Shake small particles on the food.

Steam—Cook in liquid with lid to restrain steam.

Steep—Soak in hot liquid.

Stew—Cook in liquid, usually with lid on pan.

Stir—Mix cooking ingredients with spoon.

Stir fry—Cook in small amount of oil in a pan, stirring often.

Toast—Brown on grill with direct heat or on bottom of a heated pan.

Whip—Blend vigorously with a beater, whisk or spoon.

Recipes

Meats and Main Dishes

HAMBURGER

The hamburger is an institution in our society, the basic ingredients being cooked ground beef and a sliced bun.

The meat is usually cooked on a flat heated surface, as a skillet, griddle, or wire grill over coals. It can be cooked on a heated rock, supported by a wire rack over coals, or steamed in an aluminum foil wrap.

The bun can be the typical white bakery bun or a whole wheat bun, which is my preference. In the absence of a bun, a slice or two of loaf bread can serve. Try one half of an English muffin for an open top burger. In any case, heat the bun or bread, or toast the inside of the bun with some margarine in a skillet, open Dutch oven, or a griddle.

For any hamburger to be served, consider using one or more of these:

Salad dressing
Mustard—dijon or creamy
Olives, sliced—green or ripe
Pickles—sweet, dill, or sour
Soy sauce
Cream cheese
Onions, chives
Mushrooms—cooked or raw
Tomato—sliced or garnished by cherry sized ones
Sauerkraut
Chile sauce

Peppers—bell, mild or hot
Dill weed
Parsley
Horseradish
Cheese—firm or soft, sliced or melted
Herbs—thyme, basil
Catsup
Relish—chopped, mixed pickles

MINI-BURGERS

Select the bread to be used. You can use yeast rolls, small sliced loaf bread, biscuits, or other rolls. Prepare beef patties of a size to fit the bread selection. Cook the beef patties and serve warm.

Have the support items available. Cook enough mini-burgers for several for each person.

FRANKFURTERS

Whether you call them frankfurters, franks, wieners, hot dogs, or some degree of sausage, these have been often considered a basic item for cookouts because of their convenience and utility. They are easily carried and refrigerated, and can be boiled or grilled on a griddle, open grate, spit, or stick. Sliced lengthwise or cut across in slices, they can be served in a bun, on other breads, or cooked in a common dish.

Boiling—Place franks in boiling water and cook for five or six minutes.
Griddle—Slice the franks lengthwise and brown on one side, turn them and brown the other side.
Grate—Place franks on the grate, turning occasionally to brown each side.
Spit—Insert the spit in one end and continue through the length of the frank. Cook supported over coals and turn occasionally to cook each side.

SANDWICH MELT

sliced lunchmeat
sandwich bread
sandwich spread

grated cheese
soft margarine

Place your favorite lunchmeat on one piece of sandwich bread. Place sandwich spread and grated cheese, if desired, on the other piece of bread. Place the two portions of sandwich together and spread a small amount of margarine on the outside of the bread pieces. Place the sandwich on a slightly oiled griddle, skillet or open Dutch oven. When the sandwich is toasted enough, turn the sandwich and toast the other side.

These can be served as they are toasted or can be retained in a heat retaining box. Make enough for all persons.

REUBEN SANDWICH

2 lb ground beef
16 slices rye bread
8 tsp salad dressing

8 slices cheese
1 16-oz can sauerkraut
4 tbsp margarine

Form ground beef into eight patties and cook on grill. On each of eight pieces of rye bread, place a meat patty, 1 tbsp salad dressing, a slice of cheese and a portion of the sauerkraut, then a top piece of bread to form your sandwich.

Melt some margarine on a griddle or skillet. Place the sandwich on the cooking surface until the bread browns, then turn the sandwich to brown the other side. Serves 8.

SAUCY BURGER

2 lb ground meat
1 tbsp minced onion
1 16-oz can tomato
  sauce
½ cup chopped bell
  pepper

1 cup sliced mushrooms
1 tbsp sugar
1 tbsp Worcestershire
  sauce
sandwich buns
1 cup grated cheese

Brown meat in a skillet, drain. Add onion, tomato sauce, peppers, mushrooms, sugar and Worcestershire sauce. Cook until the peppers are soft. Add small amount of water, if needed, to thin mixture.

Spoon a portion of the mixture on a bun and sprinkle with cheese, if desired. Warm buns to improve the dish. Serves 8.

CREAMED BEEF

2 2-½-oz jars chipped
  beef
12 oz milk

1 tsp parsley flakes
1 cup grated cheese
8 pieces toasted bread

Chop the beef and combine with milk, parsley, and cheese in sauce pan and cook slowly until the sauce is thick. Add 1 or 2 tbsp of flour, if desired, to thicken. Serve sauce on toasted bread or hot biscuits. Serves 8.

BEEF RIBS

3 tbsp cooking oil
3 lb of beef short ribs
  or at least one rib
  per person
3 tbsp molasses
2 tbsp vinegar

1 cup chopped celery
1 cup green peas
1 8 oz can tomato sauce
1 can beef broth
½ tsp dried thyme

Heat the cooking oil in a skillet and brown the ribs on all sides. Add the other ingredients and bake for about 2 hours or until the meat is tender. Occasionally check for adequate liquid; add small amount of water if needed.

Remove the liquid fat with a spoon. After serving the ribs, the vegetables and broth may be served over the ribs. Serves 8.

POT ROAST

1 3-lb beef roast— rolled, pot, round bone or rump cut	1 tbsp cooking oil 1 cup water garlic salt

Brown roast on each side in the oil in a skillet. Place in a baking pan, add water, and sprinkle garlic salt on top of roast.

Cook about 2 to 3 hours in oven, adding small amount of water if needed. Serves 8.

MEAT LOAF

3 lb ground beef	$1/2$ cup bell pepper,
$1 1/2$ cups cracker crumbs	chopped or 1 tbsp parsley flakes
2 eggs	$1 1/2$ tsp salt
1 8-oz can tomato sauce	$1/4$ tsp marjoram
1 onion, chopped	

Mix all ingredients; place in casserole dish or pan. Bake 1 hour in covered oven. Serves 8.

COWBOY STEW

2–3 lb ground beef 1 tbsp margarine	2 15-oz cans chili beans

Brown beef in margarine in skillet. Add beans and cook slowly 15–20 minutes in covered skillet. Serves 8.

Variation

Brown one medium onion, finely chopped, with the beef.

BEEF TIPS AND RICE

1 cup brown rice
2¼ cups water
1 tbsp cooking oil
2 tbsp margarine
1 lb sirloin steak, cubed
1 tsp minced onion

½ 11-oz can cream of
  mushroom soup
2 tbsp brown sugar
½ tsp ground basil
1 tbsp parsley flakes

Combine rice, water, and cooking oil in large sauce pan or Dutch oven, bring to a boil and cook for about 45 minutes or until the rice is done.

While the rice is cooking, melt the margarine in a skillet and brown the cubed steak and onions. Add soup, sugar, and basil and cook in the covered skillet for 10 minutes or until steak is tender. Stir in parsley flakes. If additional liquid is needed, add more soup.

Serve rice on plates and spoon cubed steak and liquid on rice. Serves 4.

CORNED BEEF AND CABBAGE

4–5 cups cabbage,
  shredded
1 11-oz can cream of
  celery soup

1 tsp minced onions
1 12-oz can corned beef

Mix cabbage, soup and onions, and place in an oiled baking pan or Dutch oven. Slice or chop corned beef and place on top of cabbage. Bake about 20 minutes or until cabbage is done. Serves 4 to 6.

SWISS STEAK

1 3-lb round steak,
  1 inch thick
3 tbsp margarine
1 tsp salt
1 large onion, chopped

3 sticks celery, chopped
$\frac{1}{2}$ cup catsup
1 tbsp dried parsley
  flakes

Brown both sides of beef in margarine in skillet. Add other ingredients and cook covered for 2 hours. Add small amount of water if needed to keep sauce thinner. Serves 8.

BEEF BAKE

2 cups macaroni
1$\frac{1}{2}$ lb ground beef
$\frac{3}{4}$ cup chopped celery
$\frac{1}{2}$ cup chopped bell pepper

1 8-oz can tomato sauce
1 cup water
$\frac{1}{2}$ tsp salt

Cook macaroni, rinse, drain and set aside. Brown the ground beef, celery and bell peppers; drain well. Add tomato sauce, water, salt and the cooked macaroni; mix well. Place the mixed ingredients in an oiled pan. Bake for 30 minutes. Serves 8.

Variations
  1. Add a 16-oz can of whole kernel corn to the mixed ingredients.
  2. Sprinkle grated cheese on the dish before baking.

QUICK CASSEROLE

1 1-oz package gravy mix
1 12-oz can roast beef
½ cup chopped celery
1 tbsp minced onion

1 4-oz can mushrooms
1 8-oz can water chestnuts
1 cup rice
2 cups water

Empty gravy package in bowl, add beef, celery, onion, mushrooms and water chestnuts. Add rice and water, stir, then place in covered skillet or oven.

Cook 30 minutes or until rice is cooked. Serves 6–8.

CHICKEN AND MUSHROOMS

1 tbsp margarine
4 oz mushrooms, sliced

1 11-oz can cream of
  mushroom soup
4 chicken breasts

Melt margarine in skillet and brown mushrooms. Place mushrooms and soup in a baking pan, then place chicken in the pan. Bake for about 40–45 minutes or until chicken is tender. Serves 4.

PIZZA

¾ lb ground beef
1 pkg pizza mix
1 4-oz can tomato sauce

¼ lb cheese, grated
olives, sliced

Brown beef in open skillet and set aside to remain warm. Mix pizza dough as directed and form into crust to fit a baking pan.

Place the ground beef and cheese on the crust; pour tomato sauce on each crust; then add sliced olives on top.

Bake as directed or about 25–30 minutes. Serves 4.

Variations
1. Use sausage instead of beef.
2. Place chopped pieces of pimiento or parsley on top of sauce.

QUICK PIZZA

For each person to be served:

1 English muffin	2 tbsp olives, sliced
1 tbsp margarine	8 slices small pepperoni
2 tbsp catsup	4 tbsp cheese, shredded

Slice each muffin, spread some margarine on one side of each half of the split muffin. Turn the spread side down and on each half muffin place catsup, olives, pepperoni, and cheese. Place muffin halves in a baking pan for oven heating or directly in the bottom of a Dutch oven. Heat the muffins in the oven for about five minutes until the muffin pizzas are warm enough. If an oven is not available, you can heat the muffin pizzas in a covered, heavy skillet.

Instead of pepperoni you can prepare ground beef or bacon. For each split muffin, brown about 2 oz ground meat, draining well, or cook two slices of bacon crisp and crumble it.

SKILLET DINNER

1 lb ground beef	1 11-oz can cream of
1 tbsp minced onions	mushroom soup
1 cup celery, diced	½ tsp salt
2 cups potatoes,	½ tsp basil
unpeeled, diced	½ tsp thyme

Brown beef in large skillet or bottom of Dutch oven, drain excess grease. Add onions and stir with meat for one minute. Add other ingredients and stir. Cover skillet or oven and cook for about 25 minutes or until potatoes are done. Serves 4 to 6.

MEAT PIE

1½ lb ground beef	½ tsp basil
2 tbsp margarine	½ tsp oregano
1 tsp minced onion	½ cup water
½ cup celery, diced	2 cups biscuit mix
½ cup green peas	

Brown ground beef in skillet, drain, and set aside. Melt margarine and brown the onions and celery. Combine beef, onions, celery, peas, basil, oregano, and water. Cover and cook for 15 minutes, place the mixture in an oiled baking dish. Mix the biscuit mix as directed, roll or pat to shape and place on top of the mixture. Bake for about 15 minutes until top crust is done. Serves 8.

BAKED EGGS

1 egg per person

Crack and pour an egg in an oiled dessert mold, foil cupcake pan or constructed foil holder. This constructed foil holder can be made of a piece of heavy aluminum foil pressed around a 10- to 12-oz can, then removed to serve as your egg holder. You may want to put cupcake papers in the mold or foil pan, then remove the egg in cupcake paper when done.

Place egg containers in the oven and bake for about 10 minutes to the consistency preferred.

You may wish to enhance the eggs by adding one of these ingredients before baking:

crumbled, crisp bacon
grated cheese
Italian seasoning
dill weed
salt, pepper

Eggs can be prepared for individual preferences.

BEEF AND EGG

1 15-oz can of corned   4 eggs
  beef hash

Divide the corned beef into four equal portions. Press the beef on the sides and bottoms of oiled dessert molds or foil cupcake pans. You may want to place cupcake papers in aluminum dessert molds and use these for holding your beef and egg. Break eggs and place one egg in each beef lined pan. Place the pans in the oven and bake for 15 minutes. Serves 4.

EGGS IN A BOX

slices of thick-slice bread   eggs
$1/2$ cup margarine

Using biscuit cutter, cut hole in center of thick-slice bread. Soften margarine and spread on each side of bread.

Place bread on a griddle until one side of bread is toasted. Turn bread over and slowly pour one egg into the hole in each piece of bread; cook eggs for about 5 minutes and remove each egg/toast with flat lifter.

GREEN STUFFED EGGS

8 eggs $1/8$ tsp garlic salt
1 avocado   1 tsp Dijon mustard
1 tbsp lemon juice

After boiling eggs, cool and peel them. Slice eggs in half and remove egg yolks.

Combine egg yolks, avocado, lemon juice and garlic salt; mash to a smooth paste. Add mustard, if desired, and mix.

Spoon the mixture into the egg halves. Serves 8.
needed. Serves 8.

OMELET

Many opinions and practices are given to the proper preparation of an omelet. The suggestions here have served me, but you may develop your preferences.

I prefer to remove the eggs from refrigeration and let them reach ambient temperature before cooking. Selection of your skillet or pan size will influence the number of eggs to use. I prefer a small skillet, such as a 6-inch diameter for two eggs or a 6- to 8-inch diameter for four eggs. You may want to use an internally-coated skillet to help prevent sticking.

Choose your omelet filling and prepare it first. You can use any one or a combination of these items for the filling:

crisp bacon, chopped
ham, diced
cheese, grated or small cubes
bell pepper, small cubes
onions, finely chopped
braised mushrooms
spinach, small pieces, braised

Melt 2 tbsp of margarine in the skillet and have the skillet hot.

Crack the eggs and place them in a small bowl, adding a couple of tablespoons of milk or water. Stir the eggs vigorously with a fork or whisk.

Pour the eggs into the skillet, having the egg mixture no thicker than 1/4 inch. As the eggs cook over low heat, use a pancake turner and lift the edge of the omelet, tilting the skillet slightly to allow some of the soft egg mix to run under the lifted edge of the cooked egg bottom. Do this on two or three places around the omelet. Repeat this to cook the entire soft, upper portion.

Place your filling on one half of the omelet and fold the other half over the filled half. You may want to place the filling in the middle third and fold both outer thirds over the middle third. For a firmer omelet, turn the omelet over for a moment of further cooking.

Serve the omelet on a warm plate. Garnish the top with parsley, dill weed, Italian seasoning, ground pepper, or other preferences.

SCRAMBLED OMELET

2 tbsp margarine	1 cup cottage cheese
8 eggs	dill weed

Melt margarine in skillet. Beat eggs and stir in cheese. Cook eggs, stirring until almost firm. Sprinkle dill weed over eggs and serve warm. Serves 4.

OVEN OMELET

2 cups 1/2-in. bread cubes	1/2 cup grated cheese
1 cup milk	1/2 tsp salt
2 tbsp margarine	parsley or dill weed
4 eggs, beaten	

Combine bread cubes and milk and soak in a mixing bowl. Melt margarine in baking pan, add eggs, cheese, salt, and bread cube mixture and stir. Bake for 15 minutes until eggs are done. Remove from oven, sprinkle parsley or dill weed on top and serve warm. Serves 4.

EGG SQUARES

4 eggs, beaten	1/4 tsp salt
1/4 cup margarine, melted	1 cup cheese, shredded
1/2 cup whole wheat flour	3/4 cup zucchini, diced
2 tsp baking powder	

Combine eggs, margarine, flour, baking powder, and salt, mix well. Stir in cheese and zucchini. Pour into oiled 8-inch square pan, bake for about 30 minutes. Remove from oven, and cut into small squares for serving.

PORK CHOPS

8 pork chops   1 can mushroom soup
2 tbsp cooking oil   1 tsp salt

Brown pork chops in oil. Add soup and salt and cook for 60 minutes in covered skillet. Serves 8.

Variations
1. Add 1 can tomato sauce.
2. Add 1 tbsp dried parsley flakes.

HAM AND SWEET POTATOES

1/4 cup margarine   8 slices ham
3/4 cup brown sugar   4 medium sweet potatoes

If the ham slices are raw, the ham should be browned in a skillet. Use a small amount of margarine and brown the ham on both sides. If the ham is precooked, it may be placed in a skillet without further cooking.

Place margarine and brown sugar in the skillet and stir until well mixed. Place the ham slices in the mixture, one slice for each person.

Peel sweet potatoes and cut the potatoes in 1/2-inch thick slices. Place the sweet potatoes in the skillet and put the lid on the skillet. Cook covered about 30–40 minutes, or until the potatoes are soft to the prongs of a fork. Serves 8.

FISH-IN-FOIL

Fish fillets, one per person
For each serving:
2 tbsp chopped celery   1 tsp dried parsley
1 thin slice of lemon   1 tbsp water

Using a sheet of heavy-duty aluminum foil, place a fillet on foil with other ingredients on fillet. Bring foil edges together and seal the foil edges by folding them twice. Make a separate foil package for each person.

Place foil packages on coals for about 5 minutes, then turn the package over for 2 or 3 minutes. Remove and check to see if the meat flakes well.

If you have adequate oven space, you can bake the foil packages in an oven for about 20 minutes.

BRAISED FISH FILLETS

4 tbsp margarine   dill weed
8 fillets

Melt 2 tbsp of margarine in skillet, place one or two fillets in a skillet. When fillet is brown, about 6 to 8 minutes, turn it to brown other side until done. Sprinkle dill weed on top and serve warm.

Add more margarine if needed for other fillets. Serves 8.

BAKED FISH FILLETS

4 tbsp margarine   1/4 cup milk or sour cream
4 fillets   parsley
2 tbsp lemon juice

Oil a baking pan, place the lemon juice and milk in pan, then place the fillets in pan. Bake in an oven for 15 to 20 minutes, check to be certain fish is done. Serve with parsley sprinkled on fillets. Serves 4.

SCALLOP CASSEROLE

16 oz scallops   2 tbsp lemon juice
1/2 11-oz can cream of   1/2 tsp thyme
  mushroom soup   1 cup cracker crumbs

Mix scallops, soup, juice, and thyme and place in an oiled baking dish. Bake for 15 minutes, sprinkle cracker crumbs on top and bake 15 additional minutes. Serves 4.

You might wish to add with the soup one slice of bacon which has been cooked until crisp and crumbled.

OYSTER CASSEROLE

1 qt oysters	4 tbsp margarine
2 cups cracker crumbs	1 cup liquid

Oil a baking pan. Place a layer of one-third of cracker crumbs on bottom of pan, then a layer of one-half of the oysters; add 2 tbsp margarine. Repeat with a layer of cracker crumbs and the other half of oysters and 2 tbsp of margarine. Place the remaining crumbs on top. Add a cup of the oyster liquid or milk and bake for about 40 minutes. Serves 6 to 8.

KIPPERED HERRING

This herring has been smoked and salted to provide a tasty fish product. Kippered herring is available in 3-oz cans.

The herring can be served from the can, served as a snack from the table,or added to sandwiches or prepared dishes. Such canned and ready-to-eat foods are excellent items for a day hike or backpacking.

SEAFOOD RICE

1½ cups brown rice	1 6-oz can crab meat
3 cups water	2 4-oz cans small shrimp
1 tbsp cooking oil	1 tbsp parsley flakes
2 tbsp olive oil	1 tsp ground basil
1 tbsp minced onion	

Combine rice, water, and oil in a large sauce pan or Dutch oven; cover and bring to a boil and cook about 45 minutes.

While the rice is cooking, place the olive oil in a skillet and brown the onions. Add the crab meat, shrimp, parsley, and basil and mix well. Stir this mixture in the rice and allow the rice to finish cooking. Serves 6 to 8.

SALMON BAKE

1 10 ¾-oz can cream
   of mushroom soup
1 15 ½ oz can salmon,
   drained
½ cup chopped celery

¼ cup sliced green
   olives
1 tbsp soy sauce
1 3-oz can of chow mein
   noodles

Combine soup, crumbled salmon, celery, olives, and soy sauce in bowl. Mix and place in oiled baking pan. Bake for 15 minutes. Add noodles and bake an additional 15 minutes. Serves 8.

Variation
Instead of noodles, prepare biscuit dough; cut and place biscuits on top of mixed ingredients.

SALMON PATTIES

1 16-oz can salmon
2 eggs
1 cup cracker crumbs

¼ cup shredded cheese
¼ tsp salt

Drain salmon, reserving liquid. Break apart salmon, remove any bones or skin, if desired. Combine all ingredients in a bowl and mix well; add some drained liquid only if needed for smooth mixture. Form mixture into patties and brown on both sides in an oiled skillet or griddle. Serves 4.

SALMON PLATE

1 16-oz can salmon   crackers

Drain salmon and place on a serving plate. Each diner can serve salmon from the plate.
You may wish to sprinkle dill weed or onion salt on your serving. Serve with crisp crackers. Serves 4.

SALMON SNACK

1 16-oz can salmon	1 tbsp Dijon mustard
½ cup salad dressing	crackers

Drain salmon. Break apart salmon, removing bones or skin, if desired. Add salad dressing and mustard. Mix well.

Spread on crackers for snacks. Add olive slices or dill weed for flavor and garnish. Serves 6 to 8.

TUNA CASSEROLE

2 12-oz cans tuna	¼ cup margarine, melted
1 cup sandwich spread	1 cup cracker crumbs

Drain tuna, mix with sandwich spread and enough margarine to provide smooth mixture. Place in an oiled baking pan and cover top with crumbs. Bake for about 20–25 minutes until hot. Serves 6–8.

TUNA SALAD

1 12-oz can tuna	4 tbsp salad dressing
¼ cup sweet pickles, chopped	2 boiled eggs, chopped

Break apart tuna in mixing bowl, add chopped pickles, salad dressing and chopped eggs and mix well. The tuna salad can be served on sandwich bread, with crackers, directly on plates or as addition to other foods. Serves 4.

Variation
Add some finely chopped celery or apples to the mixture.

Vegetables and Salads

VEGETABLE MEDLEY

For simple, colorful, and tasty dishes, serve some of the raw vegetables listed below. These can be prepared at your outdoor site or in your kitchen before your outing. If prepared earlier, place each vegetable in a plastic bag and then you can use any portion when needed. Cool the vegetables and use them when needed.

You might wish to have some dip available to complement the vegetables. You can use these for appetizers before meals or as snacks any time.

Carrots—Remove the top and any root extensions. Cut them lengthwise to the desired length, or cut crosswise and have small discs. These can be chilled in water in a tightly closed container.

Broccoli—Cut flowerets from the main stem. Slice the flowerets into desired sizes. Retain the stem for later cooking.

Cauliflower—Remove the flowered portion in small pieces, cut to desired sizes.

Bell peppers—Cut in half, remove the stem connection and seeds. The pepper can be cut in slices.

Turnips—Remove stem and bottom root extension. Slice into thin pieces.

Squash—Choose the zucchini, yellow or preferred variety. Slice crosswise into round discs.

Tomatoes—Use the small cherry tomatoes. These carry well and are easily served. Use the larger garden tomatoes, remove the stem connection and for quality serving, peel and remove the tomato skin. The tomatoes can be sliced or quartered.

SLICED AVOCADOS

4 avocados   onion salt
2 tbsp lemon juice   crackers

Peel and seed avocados, slicing in thin slices. Sprinkle lemon juice and onion salt on avocado pieces.

Serve as snacks for spreading on crackers or on a serving plate for the table. Serves 8.

CUCUMBERS IN VINEGAR

$1/2$ cup vinegar   4 medium cucumbers
$1 1/2$ cups water

Combine vinegar and water in a serving bowl. Slice cucumbers and place in the water-vinegar liquid.

This can be prepared an hour or two before the meal to allow marinating time. The dish can be served cooled or at open temperature. Serves 8.

CUCUMBER-ZUCCHINI SALAD

3 medium cucumbers   4 oz sour cream
3 medium zucchini   4 oz buttermilk

Slice cucumbers and zucchinis into a mixing bowl.

Combine sour cream and buttermilk, add to vegetables and stir well. Serves 8.

THREE-BEAN SALAD

This is an old favorite of many people. I would suggest using canned vegetables for easy preparation and convenience if storage is a problem. Fresh items, however, enhance the quality of the salad.

Several items to use are pinto beans, string beans, garbonzo beans, lima beans, and/or wax beans. Consider any bean or pea that will be firm. Use a 16-oz can of three of these choices, drained.

For a clear sauce use a blend of 4 tbsp of sugar and 4 tbsp of white vinegar. You can add a dash of basil or onion salt to the dish.
Prepare the dish ahead and cool it for a few hours before the meal. Serves 8.

WARM SPINACH SALAD

4 oz spinach
8 mushrooms
2 tbsp margarine

$\frac{1}{4}$ cup cheese salad
dressing

Chop spinach into small pieces and slice mushrooms. Melt margarine in a skillet, stir spinach and mushrooms in the skillet until well warmed, then stir in salad dressing for a few minutes. Serve on warm plates. Serves 4.

BRAISED MUSHROOMS

2-4 tbsp margarine   1 lb mushrooms

Melt margarine in skillet. Slice the mushrooms from base through the crown; if mushrooms are small, you may wish to leave them whole.
Place mushrooms in skillet and stir occasionally until they are browned sufficiently. Serve warm. Serves 8.

STEAMED CABBAGE

2 medium heads cabbage
1 tsp salt

1 cup water
vinegar

Cut heads of cabbage in quarters; place in salted boiling water. Cover and cook 10–15 minutes. Test for tenderness; do not overcook. Individuals can season with vinegar to taste. Serves 8.

SKILLET CABBAGE

2 tbsp margarine   ¼ tsp onion salt
6 cups cabbage, shredded   4 tbsp water
1 cup celery, chopped

Melt margarine in a large skillet, add cabbage, celery, onion salt and water. Stir well, place lid on skillet and cook about 10 minutes, stirring occasionally. Do not overcook, serve warm. Serves 6 to 8.

You may wish to add 1 tsp of soy sauce or Worcestershire sauce with the onion salt.

CORN ON THE COB

1 ear corn per person   boiling water
1 tsp salt

Remove shucks and silk from ears. Place corn in pan; add salt and enough boiling water to cover corn. Cover and bring to a boil; cook 6–8 minutes. Puncture corn grains with knife tip for tenderness test.

DILLED CARROTS

4 tbsp margarine   2 tbsp chopped fresh dill
4 cups sliced carrots   or 1 tbsp dried dill weed
½ cup water

Melt margarine in heavy pan. Add carrots, water, dill and stir to mix. Cover and cook for about 10 minutes. Serves 8.

STIRRED VEGETABLES

¼ cup margarine   1 cup carrots, sliced
½ cup chopped onion   1 tsp garlic salt
2 cups cauliflower   1 tsp parsley
2 cups zucchini,   ½ tsp chopped basil
   sliced

Melt margarine in bottom of pan. Brown onion, add other ingredients, and stir occasionally for 5 minutes. Cover and cook about 5 minutes or until done. Serves 8.

Variation
Sprinkle with dill weed.

DEEP DISH EGGPLANT

2 lb ground beef	2 8-oz cans tomato sauce
3 tbsp margarine	1/4 tsp oregano
1 tbsp minced onion	1/2 cup chopped olives
2 small eggplants	1 1/2 cups grated firm cheese

Brown the ground beef in a skillet, drain and set aside. Melt margarine in a deep skillet, brown onions, then add cooked ground beef. Peel and cube the eggplants and add to cooking container. Put tomato sauce and oregano in container and stir. Cook covered for about 20 minutes until eggplant is tender. Sprinkle olives and cheese on top of cooked food and heat for about 5 minutes until cheese is well melted. Add a small amount of water if needed. Serves 8.

SKILLET EGGPLANT

2 tbsp margarine	1/2 tsp salt
1 small onion, chopped	1/4 cup water
2 cups eggplant, peeled and diced	1/2 tsp ground basil
1 large tomato, diced	

Melt margarine and brown onion. Add other ingredients, stir, cover and simmer about 20 to 25 minutes, until eggplant is tender. Add small amount of water if needed. Serves 4.

FOIL SQUASH

¼ cup margarine	2 cups yellow squash,
½ tsp thyme	sliced
½ tsp salt	2 cups zucchini, sliced

Melt margarine in small pan: add thyme and salt. Place the sliced squash on a large sheet of foil and pour the seasoned margarine over the squash. Fold the foil on the edges and place the foil on coals. For ease of handling, the ingredients can be divided and placed in two foil packages. Cook on one side about 10 minutes then turn the package over to cook the other side about 5 minutes. Serves 6 to 8.

LENTIL-RICE STEW

2 tbsp margarine	1 can beef soup
¼ cup minced onion	¾ cup brown rice (not
1 cup diced celery	minute or processed)
6 cups water	1½ tsp garlic salt
1 cup dried lentils	½ tsp chopped basil
¾ cup diced carrots	½ tsp oregano

Melt margarine ; stir and brown onions and celery. Add water and lentils. Cover and bring to a boil; cook 20 minutes. Add other ingredients, bring to a boil and cook 1 hour or until rice is done. A small amount of water may be added, if necessary. Serves 6–8

VEGETABLE STEW

1 lb ground beef	1 cup chopped bell peppers
2 cups chopped celery	1 tsp salt
1 cup chopped onions	1 tsp sugar
2 cups sliced zucchini	1 tsp Italian seasoning
1 cup sliced yellow	½ tsp chopped basil
squash	
2 16-oz cans tomatoes	

Brown beef, celery, and onion in a sauce pan; drain well. Add zucchini, squash, tomatoes, bell peppers, and seasonings. Cover with lid and cook 30–40 minutes until vegetables are tender. Add small amount of water, if needed. Serves 8.

CANDIED SWEET POTATOES

8 sweet potatoes
1 cup brown sugar

1 tbsp lemon juice
4 tbsp margarine

Place potatoes in boiling water and cook about 30 minutes until tender. Peel potatoes and slice into $1/2$ -inch thick pieces. Place half of the potato pieces in a baking pan, sprinkle with half of the sugar. Place remaining potato pieces in pan and spread the remaining sugar, lemon juice and margarine over the top of potatoes. Bake about 20 minutes. Serves 8.

BAKED SWEET POTATOES

1 sweet potato per person

Wash potatoes and prick the top side of each with a knife blade. Place potatoes in an oven and bake for 45 minutes, or until soft.
Serve a potato to each person. Place some margarine on the warm potato.

MACARONI WITH CHEESE

1 cup elbow macaroni
2 qt boiling water
1 11-oz can cream of
  celery soup

1 cup cottage cheese
2 tsp basil
$1/2$ cup Parmesan cheese

Cook macaroni in boiling water for about 8 minutes and drain. In an oiled baking pan combine macaroni, soup, cottage cheese and basil. Mix well. Sprinkle Parmesan cheese on top and bake about 20 minutes. Serves 4 to 6.

BAKED POTATOES

1 potato per person

Wash the outside of the potatoes, and puncture a small hole on two sides of each potato. Place the potatoes in the oven and bake about 1 hour. The time will vary depending on the size of the potatoes.

OZARK BAKED BEANS

2 cups dried white beans	1 tsp dry mustard
1½ qts water	¼ cup molasses
1 tsp salt	¼ lb salt pork, sliced
⅓ cup brown sugar	1 large onion, diced

Place beans in water and soak overnight.
Add salt and cook for 1 hour or until tender. Drain liquid into a separate pan. Add other ingredients and 2 cups of drained liquid to beans. Cover and bake for 4–5 hours. Check occasionally, adding small amounts of water if needed. Serves 8.

NAVY BEANS

2 cups navy beans	1 tsp salt
6 cups water	1 tsp onion salt
¼ lb bacon, crisp	

Place beans in water and soak overnight. Chop bacon into small pieces and cook in a skillet until crisp, drain. Combine all the ingredients in a large cooking pot, cover and cook for 1 ½ to 2 hours. Serves 8.

PINTO BEANS

2 cups beans, dried	1 tsp onion salt
6 cups water	1 oz salt pork, sliced

Place beans in water and soak overnight. Put onion salt and pork in beans; cover and cook 3 hours. Add small amounts of water if needed. Serves 8.

SUCCOTASH

1 cup dried lima beans	1/2 tsp salt
3 cups water	1 12-oz can whole kernel
1 oz salt pork, diced	corn or fresh corn

Cover beans with water and soak overnight; then drain.

Place beans, pork, salt, and enough water to cover in a sauce pan. Cook covered over low fire for 1 1/2 hours; add small amount of water if needed. Add corn; stir and cook 1/2 hour. Serves 8.

BAKED CORN

1 16-oz can cream style corn	1 tsp garlic salt
1 16-oz can whole kernel corn	2 cups grated cheese
	1 tsp baking powder
	1/4 cup cooking oil
1/2 cup corn meal	2 eggs, beaten

Combine corn, corn meal, garlic salt, cheese, baking powder and cooking oil. Beat eggs and add to mixture. Place mixture in baking pan in oven.

Bake 40–50 minutes. Serves 8.

Variation

Add 4-oz can chopped chilies or 1/2 cup chopped bell peppers.

MUSHROOM-POTATO CASSEROLE

2 tbsp margarine	4 cups potatoes, sliced
1 lb fresh mushrooms	thinly
1/2 cup Parmesan cheese	4 tbsp margarine
2 tbsp flour	1 cup milk
1/4 tsp salt	1/2 cup cracker crumbs

Melt 2 tbsp margarine in skillet and saute mushrooms, setting aside. Mix the cheese, flour and salt in a pan, setting aside. Place 2 cups of the sliced potatoes in an oiled baking pan, then place one-half of the mushrooms and one-half the cheese mix on top. Place the remaining 2 cups of potatoes in the pan and then the remaining mushrooms and cheese mix on next. Pour the milk in the baking pan and sprinkle the cracker crumbs on top.

Bake for 60 minutes, checking to assure the potatoes are done. Serves 8.

NOODLE CASSEROLE

1 lb noodles	1 can mushroom soup
2 lb ground beef	1 can peas
1 medium onion, chopped	1 tsp salt
2 tbsp cooking oil	1/2 tsp oregano

Cook noodles in a separate pan by directions on package; drain. Brown meat and onion in oil in skillet; then add soup, peas and seasoning. Place noodles and meat mixture together in pan. Place in oven and bake 1/2 hour. Serves 8.

NOODLE BAKE

1 lb noodles	1 tsp salt
2 cups yogurt	1 cup cracker crumbs
2 eggs, beaten	

Cook noodles; then place them in an oiled baking pan. Mix yogurt, eggs, and salt in a bowl and pour over the noodles. Sprinkle cracker crumbs on top.

Bake about 15 minutes. Serves 8.

EGGPLANT AND CHEESE

1 medium eggplant	2 tsp ground basil
2 tomatoes	1/2 cup cooking oil
1 tsp minced onions	1 1/2 cup mozzarella
1 tsp salt	cheese, diced
	1 cup cracker crumbs

Peel and cut eggplant across in 3/8-in. slices. Peel and slice tomatoes. Place eggplants and tomatoes in alternating layers in an oiled baking pan. Combine onions, salt and basil in the oil and stir well, then pour the mixture over the eggplant and tomatoes.

Bake in an oven for about 30 minutes and remove to determine that eggplant is tender. Sprinkle cheese and crumbs on top of dish and place in oven for about 6 to 8 minutes, or enough time to melt the cheese. Serves 4.

SQUASH BAKE

4 tbsp margarine	1/4 lb cheese, grated
2 lbs yellow squash	1 cup cracker crumbs
1/4 tsp salt	

Melt margarine and place in oiled baking dish. Place sliced squash and salt in margarine; place cheese and then cracker crumbs on top.

Bake for about 10 minutes until tender to fork. Do not overcook. Serves 8.

Variation

Sprinkle Italian seasoning with the cracker crumbs.

HERBED POTATOES

3 lb potatoes
3 cups boiling water
1 can cream of mushroom
   soup
1 tsp basil

½ tsp marjoram
2 tbsp margarine
1 cup cracker crumbs
1 tbsp Parmesan cheese

Peel and cube potatoes. In a pan place potatoes in the boiling water; cook about 12–15 minutes until potatoes are almost soft. Drain water and place potatoes in an oiled baking pan.

In a separate pan mix the soup, basil and marjoram. Heat the mixture for 4–5 minutes and pour it over the potatoes.

In another pan melt the margarine, stir in the cracker crumbs and cheese. Pour this mixture over the potatoes.

Bake about 15 minutes. Serves 8.

VEGETABLE-CHEESE CASSEROLE

2 medium eggplants
4 cups boiling, salted
   water
1 egg
1 cup cottage cheese
1 tbsp Italian seasoning

1 10¾-can cream of
   mushroom soup
4 oz mozzarella or soft
   cheese
1 cup cracker crumbs

Wash and peel eggplants; cut into cubes. Place eggplant in a pan of boiling water; cover and cook about five minutes until tender. Drain water and place eggplant in an oiled pan. Beat egg; stir egg, cottage cheese, seasoning, and soup with eggplant. Slice soft cheese on top, sprinkle on cracker crumbs and bake for about 30 minutes. Serves 8.

Variation

Use 8-oz can of tomato sauce instead of mushroom soup.

BACON-SPINACH PIE

1 9-inch pie crust	1/2 cup cracker crumbs
1/2 lb bacon	3 eggs
1 cup cheese, grated	1 1/2 cups milk
1 10-oz package of spinach	
or 1 can spinach, drained	

Prepare pie crust, bake for 5 minutes and set aside. Cook bacon until crisp; drain and crumble. Mix bacon, cheese, spinach, and cracker crumbs. Beat eggs; combine with milk, and add to mixed ingredients. Pour mixture into the pie crust.

Bake pie 50–60 minutes in oven. Remove pie from oven and cool 15 minutes. Serves 6–8.

Variation
Add sliced mushrooms to mixture.

ZUCCHINI BAKE

1 cup brown rice	2 cups sour cream or
3 medium zucchini squash	yogurt
1 large tomato	1 tsp garlic salt
1/2 lb cheese	1 tsp oregano
	1 tbsp parsley

Cook brown rice and place in oiled pan. Slice zucchini and tomato; place on top of rice. Grate cheese and sprinkle on top. Mix sour cream, garlic and oregano and pour on top.

Bake 30 minutes. Remove and sprinkle on chopped parsley. Serves 8.

ZUCCHINI-CHEESE CASSEROLE

2 tbsp margarine, melted
3 zucchinis, cubed
2 tomatoes, cubed
1 lb cottage cheese

1 tsp basil
$\frac{1}{2}$ tsp oregano
$\frac{1}{3}$ cup Parmesan cheese
$\frac{1}{3}$ cup cracker crumbs

Combine margarine, zucchini, tomatoes, cottage cheese, basil, and oregano. Stir well and pour into an oiled baking pan. Mix Parmesan cheese and cracker crumbs and sprinkle on top of the mixture. Bake for about 30 minutes. Serves 6 to 8.

GRITS

4 cups boiling water
1 tsp salt

1 cup quick grits

Boil water, add salt, and slowly add and stir grits into the water. Heat water to boiling and cook over simmering fire for about 5 minutes, stirring often. Serves 4–6.

The grits can be served with margarine or gravy. The grits can be served as a cereal with sugar and milk.

CHEESE GRITS

6 cups boiling water
1 tsp salt
$1\frac{1}{2}$ cups grits

$\frac{1}{2}$ cup margarine
1 lb grated cheese
3 eggs

Stir grits into salted, boiling water for 5 minutes. Add margarine and cheese; stir and remove to cool for 5 minutes. Beat eggs and stir into grits.

Place in oiled baking dish and bake for 40 minutes. Serves 8.

Variations

1. Add 2 tbsp chopped pimento with the cheese.
2. Add 2 tbsp chopped bell pepper with the cheese.

STEAMED RICE

3 cups water   1 tsp salt
1½ cups rice   1 tbsp cooking oil

Bring water to a boil. Add other ingredients. Cover and cook over low heat about 20–25 minutes or until water is absorbed. Serves 8.

FLAVORED RICE

1 11-oz can beef broth   2 cups brown rice
1½ cups water   parsley flakes
1 tbsp margarine

Pour broth, water, margarine, and rice in covered deep skillet or sauce pan. Bring to a boil and cook for about 45 minutes or until rice is done. Sprinkle a few parsley flakes on the rice and heat for 5 more minutes. Serves 8.

Variation
Add 8 oz water chestnuts or 4 oz slivered almonds with the parsley.

RICE AND CORNED BEEF

1½ cups brown rice   ½ tsp salt
3 cups water   2 12-oz cans corned beef

Place rice, water, and salt in sauce pan, cover and cook for 30 minutes. Slice corned beef, place on top of rice and cook for 15 more minutes or until rice is done. Serves 8.

SPANISH RICE

1/4 cup margarine	1 1/2 cups water
1 tbsp minced onion	1 tsp salt
1/2 cup celery, diced	1 tbsp sugar
1 cup brown rice	1/2 tsp chili powder
1 8-oz can tomato sauce	1/4 cup bell pepper, diced

Melt margarine in heavy sauce pan. Add onion and celery and brown for a few minutes. Add other ingredients, stir, cover and cook for about one hour or until rice is soft. Serves 8.

You may brown a pound of ground beef in a separate skillet, drain well. Add this when the tomato sauce is included.

RICE WITH VEGETABLES

1 cup brown rice	1 cup squash, sliced
1/2 tsp salt	1/2 cup celery, diced
1 tbsp margarine	2 tbsp chopped onions
2 cups water	1 4-oz can water chestnuts
2 tsp margarine	

Place rice, salt, margarine, and water in sauce pan. Cover and cook about one hour or until water is absorbed.

Melt other margarine in skillet, brown squash, celery and onions. Remove from fire and add water chestnuts. Combine all ingredients in a serving bowl. Serves 4.

FETTUCINI NOODLES

1 lb fettucini noodles	6 tbsp margarine, melted
boiling water	1 cup Parmesan cheese

Cook noodles as directed on package. Drain noodles and place in serving bowl, stir in margarine and cheese. Serve warm. Serves 8.

PASTA SALAD

4 cups corkscrew spinach
  and tomato pasta
Sauce:
$\frac{2}{3}$ cup cooking oil
$\frac{1}{2}$ cup red vinegar

1 cup ripe olives, sliced
2 tbsp parsley flakes

$\frac{1}{2}$ tsp ground basil
$\frac{1}{2}$ tsp thyme

Cook pasta by directions on package. Combine with olives and parsley. Prepare sauce ingredients, blend well and pour over pasta mix. Serves 6–8.

Prepare this before the meal and let it marinate before serving. It can be served cooled or at open temperature.

SCALLOPED POTATOES

6 cups potatoes, sliced
4 tbsp margarine, melted
1 tsp salt

1$\frac{1}{2}$ cups milk
1 cup cracker crumbs

Place potatoes in oiled baking dish. Add salt with margarine, then add milk. Bake about 40 minutes, check for doneness. Add cracker crumbs to top and bake a few more minutes until potatoes are done. Serves 8.

Variation
Mix 2 tbsp of Parmesan cheese with the cracker crumbs.

CRACKED WHEAT

1 cup cracked wheat	2 cups water
1/2 tsp salt	honey or brown sugar
1 tbsp margarine	

Placed cracked wheat, salt, margarine, and water in sauce pan. Cover and cook about 20 to 25 minutes until water is absorbed. Stir often. Serve in cups or bowls, sweeten with honey or brown sugar. Serves 4.

Variation
Raisins or small pieces of fresh fruit can be added when served.

PEANUT BUTTER-BANANA SPREAD

peanut butter   ripe bananas

Remove peels and mash a cup full of bananas. Add small amounts of peanut butter to a mixing bowl and mix the bananas and peanut butter. Add additional peanut butter until your preferable mixture is obtained. Prepare enough mixture for the people to be served.

Spread the mixture on slices of bread and serve as sandwiches. You can also spread the mixture on crackers.

PEANUT BUTTER-HONEY SPREAD

1 cup peanut butter   1 cup honey

Place the peanut butter in a mixing bowl, add a portion of the honey and mix well. Add additional portions of the honey until the desired thickness of the mix is obtained. The mixture ratio is imprecise and will vary depending on the consistency of the peanut butter and the honey and also your choice of spreadability.

Use the mixture to spread on bread for sandwiches or on crackers for snack use. You can place the spread in a wide mouth, screw lidded jar for storage and occasional use.

SUGARED FRUIT

This is a serving that is very flexible to use when fresh fruit is available. Choose whole fruit such as blueberries, blackberries, cherries, or seedless grapes. Or slice some bananas, strawberries, melon, peaches, or figs. The fruit is placed in the serving container and sprinkled with powdered sugar. The fruit can be placed in individual cups or bowls, or it can be served by individuals from a large container. If the fruit is moist from being sliced or removed from a cooler, the sugar will adhere better.

If fresh fruit is not available, you choose canned fruit. Usually little sugar will be needed because of the amount added in canning, but you can garnish the fruit with sprinkled powdered sugar.

FRUIT SALAD

1 29-oz can peaches
1 29-oz can pineapple
  chunks
1 16-oz can white grapes
1 8-oz can maraschino
  cherries

½ cup raisins
8 oz small marshmallows
powdered sugar

Drain juice from fruit and retain. Combine fruit and marshmallows in a bowl and mix well. Add small amount of the juice if needed for a moist mix; sprinkle a small amount of powdered sugar on top of the mixed fruit for garnish. Serves 8.

This may be served at surrounding temperature or cooled in your ice box, if desired. If fresh fruits are available, you may wish to use them in the salad.

Soups

CLAM CHOWDER

2 slices bacon
2 tsp margarine
1 bell pepper, diced
1 tsp onion salt

2 11-oz cans cream of
  mushroom soup
4 potatoes, diced
4 6-oz cans minced clams

Dice and brown bacon in a skillet, drain and set bacon aside. Melt margarine in a skillet and brown bell pepper. Into a large sauce pan place bacon, bell peppers, onion salt, mushroom soup, potatoes and clams. Cover, bring to a boil, simmer for about 20 minutes until potatoes are soft. Add water if needed for thinning. Serves 8.

CRAB MEAT CHOWDER

1 11-oz can cream of
  mushroom soup
1 11-oz can pea soup

1 cup milk
2 6-oz cans crab meat
1 6-oz can small shrimp

Place both cans of soup and milk in a sauce pan, stir and heat over low fire. Stir in crab meat and shrimp and heat thoroughly. Serves 6.

FISH CHOWDER

3 tbsp cooking oil
1/4 cup chopped onion
1/2 cup chopped bell
 pepper
1 cup chopped celery
1/2 cup chopped carrots
1 cup water

1 tsp salt
1/4 tsp thyme
1/4 tsp chopped basil
1 tbsp parsley
2 lbs fish fillets, cut in
 small pieces

Heat cooking oil, brown onion, bell pepper, celery and carrots. Add water, salt, thyme, basil, and parsley. Cover and cook for 20 minutes. Add fish and cook about 10 minutes or until fish is done. Serves 8.

QUICK SCALLOP CHOWDER

1 11-oz can cream of
 mushroom soup
3/4 lb bay scallops

1 cup water
2 potatoes, diced
1 tsp chopped basil

Combine all ingredients in a covered sauce pan. Cook on low heat about 20 minutes until potatoes are soft. Serves 4.

QUICK SHRIMP CHOWDER

1 11-oz can cream of
 mushroom soup
2 4 1/2 -oz cans small shrimp

2 potatoes, diced
1 tsp ground basil

Combine all ingredients in a covered sauce pan and cook about 20 minutes until the diced potatoes are soft. Serve warm. Serves 3 to 4.

GUMBO

2 lbs beef
4 tsp margarine
1 tsp salt
2 qts water
1 large onion, chopped
1 16-oz can tomatoes

1 large bell pepper
chopped
1 10-oz pkg frozen okra
1 tsp thyme
1 tsp tarragon
1 bay leaf

Cut meat into small cubes; brown in margarine in skillet. Place meat, salt, water, and chopped onion in large sauce pan and cook 1 hour.

Add tomatoes, bell pepper, okra, thyme, tarragon, and bay leaf and cook slowly for 1 hour. Serves 8.

Variation

Gulf Coast Gumbo: Use fish, shrimp or crab meat instead of beef. Add 1 tsp gumbo file.

BEAN SOUP

2 cups navy beans
8 cups water
1 tsp salt

1 tbsp minced onion
1/4 cup carrots, shredded
2 tbsp parsley

Place beans in water and soak overnight. Combine beans and water with salt, onions and carrots in a large cooking pot, cover and cook about 2 hours. Take a potato masher and thoroughly mash the beans. Add parsley and cook 15 minutes. Serves 8.

MINESTRONE SOUP

2 tbsp margarine
1 tsp minced onions
1/2 cup celery, diced
2 11-oz cans beef broth
1 16-oz can tomatoes
2 cups water

1 cup lima beans
1/2 tsp ground basil
1/2 tsp oregano
1 tbsp parsley flakes
1 cup zucchini, diced
1/2 cup elbow macaroni

Melt margarine in skillet and brown the onions and celery. In a large sauce pan or Dutch oven, place the onions, celery, beef broth, tomatoes, water, and lima beans; bring to a boil and simmer 30 minutes. Add basil, oregano, parsley, zucchini, and macaroni; again bring to a boil and cook about 10 minutes until vegetables and macaroni are done. Serves 8.

MUSHROOM BARLEY SOUP

4 tbsp margarine	2 11-oz can beef broth
1 tsp minced onion	1 cup water
1½ lb fresh mushrooms, chopped	½ cup barley
	1 tsp thyme

Melt margarine in deep skillet, brown onions and add chopped mushrooms. Cook until mushrooms are soft, then add beef broth, water, barley and thyme. Cook about one hour or until barley is tender. Add small amount of water, if needed. Serves 8.

POTATO SOUP

2 tbsp margarine	2 cups water
1 cup diced celery	3 cups milk
¼ cup chopped onion	2 tsp salt
4 cups diced potatoes	2 tbsp parsley

Melt margarine and brown the celery and onions. Add potatoes and water; cover and cook for about 1 hour. Mash vegetables for smoothness. Add milk, salt and parsley, and simmer again for 15 minutes. Serves 8.

Variations
1. Add finely chopped carrots.
2. Add finely chopped ham.

SPLIT PEA SOUP

2 cups dry split peas	1 small onion, chopped
1/4 lb bacon	1 tsp salt

Place peas in 2 1/2 cups water and soak overnight. Brown bacon in a skillet, drain and crumble. Add bacon, salt, and onion to peas; cover and cook over slow fire for 1 hour.

Inspect occasionally, adding small amounts of water, if needed, to thin soup while it cooks. Serve with crackers. Serves 8.

VEGETABLE SOUP

1 lb ground beef, optional	1/2 cup lima beans
1 tbsp margarine	1/2 cup carrots, diced
1 bell pepper, seeded	1 tsp thyme
and diced	1 tsp ground basil
1 tbsp minced onion	1 tsp salt
8 cups water	1 cup green peas
1/4 cup barley	1 cup shell macaroni

If ground beef is desired, brown the beef in a skillet, drain off the grease and set aside. In a large sauce pan or Dutch oven, melt the margarine and brown the bell pepper and onion. Add beef, water, barley, beans, carrots, thyme, basil, and salt and simmer 60 minutes. Add peas and macaroni and cook 30 minutes. Serves 8.

Other ingredients can be added, if desired. You might wish to use 3/4 cup of diced white potatoes rather than the barley. You might wish to add a cup of stewed tomatoes. Additional water can be added, if needed.

Sauces

BUTTERMILK SAUCE

1 cup buttermilk
1/2 cup salad dressing
1/2 tsp ground basil

1/2 tsp garlic salt
1/2 tsp thyme

Place ingredients in a small mixing bowl and mix well, add a little more salad dressing if a thicker mix is desired. This sauce can be prepared ahead and refrigerated until needed.

Use the dressing on salads or raw vegetable servings.

COLE SLAW SAUCE

1 5-oz can evaporated
  milk
1/4 cup vinegar

1/2 cup sour cream
1/2 tsp salt
1 tsp celery seeds

Mix ingredients in bowl. Add to shredded cabbage in amounts needed.

CHEESE SAUCE

2 tbsp margarine   1 cup milk
1 tbsp flour   ¾ cup grated cheese

Melt margarine in sauce pan, mix in flour and add milk. Cook until warm and add cheese. Cook and stir until smooth. To thin the sauce, add 1 tbsp of milk and stir well. To thicken the sauce, add 1 tbsp flour and stir to smooth consistency.

Use the sauce to pour a small amount on meat or vegetable dishes.

OIL AND VINEGAR DRESSING

4 tbsp cooking oil   1 tsp ground basil
3 tbsp red vinegar

Mix the ingredients and use to pour on vegetable salads. You may add ¼ tsp celery seeds for added flavor.

WHITE SAUCE

2 tbsp margarine   1 cup milk
2 tbsp flour

Melt margarine in sauce pan, add flour and stir until smooth. Add milk and continue stirring until sauce is thickened. The amount of flour or milk can be varied to change thickness of sauce.

BARBEQUE SAUCE

1 tbsp margarine   2 tbsp brown sugar
1 tbsp minced onions   ½ tsp dry mustard
1 8-oz can tomato sauce   1 tsp Worcestershire sauce
1 tbsp vinegar   ⅛ tsp garlic salt

Melt margarine in skillet and brown the onions. Combine the onions and other ingredients in a sauce pan. Cook over low heat for 10 minutes.

Use this sauce to brush on grilled meat.

BASTING SAUCE

1/3 cup soy sauce	3 cloves garlic, crushed
2 tbsp sugar	1 tsp ginger
1/4 cup cooking oil	

Combine ingredients and use as a sauce to baste meat that is grilled.

HORSERADISH SAUCE

1 cup sour cream	1 tbsp chopped chives,
2 tbsp horseradish	optional

Mix the sour cream and horseradish. This can serve well with a meat dish. Add the chopped chives for color and additional flavor to the sauce.

This can be prepared earlier and kept in your cooler for later use.

ITALIAN SAUCE

1 cup cooking oil	1/8 tsp marjoram
1/4 cup vinegar	1/8 tsp oregano
1 tbsp lemon juice	1/2 tsp salt
1/4 tsp dry mustard	1/4 tsp garlic salt

Add all ingredients to screw lid jar. Shake to blend.

MUSTARD SAUCE

1 cup sour cream
3 tbsp Dijon mustard

1 tbsp red vinegar,
optional

Mix the sour cream and mustard. This can serve with a meat dish or sandwich. Add the vinegar for thinning or tartness.

You may use salad dressing or mayonnaise as a substitute for the sour cream.

DESSERT SAUCE

1/2 cup sugar
1 tbsp cornstarch
1 cup water

3 tbsp margarine
2 tbsp lemon juice

Combine sugar, cornstarch, and water in pan. Stir mixture over low fire until thickened; remove from heat. Add margarine and lemon juice, stirring until sauce is smooth. Pour sauce on dessert.

Variations

1. Instead of lemon juice, use orange juice, cherry juice or a flavoring.

2. Add a few raisins to the sauce.

POPPY SEED SAUCE

1/2 cup sugar
1/4 cup vinegar
1/2 cup cooking oil

1/4 tsp salt
1/2 tsp dry mustard
2 tsp poppy seeds

Combine sugar, vinegar, oil, salt, and mustard, beat well. Add poppy seeds and stir well.

Use this sauce on fruit salads.

BATTER DIP

1 egg
½ tsp salt

½ cup milk or water
½ cup flour

Beat ingredients in mixing bowl. Dip your food in this mix and cook in cooking oil.

FRENCH TOAST BATTER

8 eggs, beaten
2 cups milk
½ tsp salt
bread

margarine
syrup, jelly or powdered
   sugar

Place eggs, milk, and salt in bowl and mix thoroughly. Dip slices of bread in the batter mix and then brown on slightly oiled griddle. Turn once and brown on other side.

Serve hot with warm syrup, jelly or powdered sugar.

Breads

BISCUITS

3 cups flour	6 tbsp cooking oil
6 tsp baking powder	1 cup milk
1/2 tsp salt	

Mix all ingredients. Roll on flat, floured surface; cut out and place in a baking pan in the oven. The biscuits can be placed directly on the bottom of a Dutch oven.

Bake about 15 minutes. Makes about 30 biscuits.

BISCUITS

Mix 3 cups biscuit mix as directed and pat out on floured, flat surface. Cut biscuits with a small open-end can and place biscuits in a baking pan in the oven. The biscuits can be placed directly on the bottom of a Dutch oven. Bake about 15 minutes.

Instead of using a flat surface, you may use floured hands and roll dough into 1 1/2 -inch balls. Then flatten into biscuit shape and place in oven.

For drop biscuits, the mixed dough can be spooned on the baking pan without any shaping.

BACON BISCUITS

¼ lb bacon   3 cups biscuit mix
1 cups milk or water

Cook bacon in a skillet to crisp condition, drain and chop bacon to very small pieces. Add the bacon pieces to the dry biscuit mix, add liquid and prepare biscuits. Cook 12–15 minutes and serve warm. Makes about 20 biscuits.

REFRIGERATED BISCUITS

These rolls of refrigerated biscuits can be a ready source of quick, warm bread for a meal. You can place the biscuits close together in an oiled baking pan and cook about 10 minutes in your oven.

There are other uses of the biscuits, which can provide variations for your meals. Handling dough is easier if you rub cooking oil on your hands. Oil the baking pan to contain the biscuits. Enhance your meals with some of these:

Cheese rolls—Flatten each biscuit to a round piece about 4 inches in diameter and place a small piece of cheddar cheese in the middle. Fold one half of the round dough over, sealing the joined edges.

Cinnamon rolls—Flatten each biscuit to a round piece about 4 inches in diameter and sprinkle the center area with cinnamon and sugar. Fold one half of the dough over, sealing the edges.

Raisin rolls—Prepare the cinnamon rolls above and place several raisins in the center of the dough, then fold the dough.

Parmesan tops—Place the biscuits close together in an oiled baking pan. Brush the tops of the biscuits with melted margarine, then sprinkle Parmesan cheese on tops of the biscuits.

Dilled tops—Place the biscuits close together in an oiled baking pan. Brush the tops of the biscuits with melted margarine, then sprinkle dill weed on the tops of the biscuits.

Seed sticks—Take each biscuit and roll into a narrow dough stick about 5 inches long. Brush the sticks in margarine and roll them in sesame, dill, anise or poppy seeds and place the sticks in an oiled baking pan.

Shaped biscuits—Shape the biscuits in square or triangle shapes, place them in the oiled baking pan.

STUFFED BISCUITS

Prepare your stuffing food first:

Sausage link—Cut small links to fit in the biscuits or longer to extend out of the biscuits, if desired. Large links can be cut across the link section to provide slices for the biscuits.

Patties—Cook sausage or ground beef to coin sizes to fit in the biscuits.

Ham square—Can be cut to fit in the biscuits.

Chipped beef—Can be chopped well and mixed with a beaten egg.

Mix biscuit dough by regular recipe and pat out or roll to a thickness of about 1/4 inch or one half your usual thickness of biscuit dough. Using a knife blade, cut the dough into rectangular shapes about 1 1/2 inches by 3 inches.

Place a portion of your meat stuffing on the dough piece and fold the dough over to make a square biscuit shape.

CORNBREAD

2 cups cornmeal   1 1/4 cups milk
1 tbsp baking powder   2 eggs, beaten
1 tsp salt   1 tbsp cooking oil
4 tbsp flour

Mix the corn meal, baking powder, salt, and flour; then add milk and mix. Add eggs and oil, stir. Pour into oiled muffin pans or cupcake holders or onto bottom of Dutch oven.

Bake 20–30 minutes. Serves 8.

Variation

Spanish Corn Bread: Add pieces of chopped pimento or bell pepper to mix.

HOT WATER PONE BREAD

2 cups corn meal
1 tsp salt
3 tbsp margarine

1½ cups boiling water
cooking oil

Mix corn meal, salt, and margarine. Add the boiling water (water *must* be boiling). Stir the ingredients; wet your hands and shape mixture into pones or patties about biscuit size and ½-inch thick.

Fry in cooking oil until golden, turn once; remove and drain. Serve hot. Serves 8.

BUNCH OF ROLLS

1 16-oz hot roll mix

¼ cup margarine, melted

Prepare hot roll dough as directed in instructions. Oil a deep baking pan or Dutch oven. When the dough is ready to be divided for rolls, pinch off pieces of dough and form into dough balls about 1 inch in size and place the balls in the baking container. Oil your hands to prepare the dough balls. When the dough balls have risen adequately bake about 20 minutes. Serves 4 to 6.

STUFFED ROLLS

½ lb ground beef
½ cup catsup
1 tsp oregano
1 tsp ground basil
1 16-oz hot roll mix
1 cup warm water

1 egg beaten
8 oz mozzarella cheese,
   grated
2 tbsp margarine, melted
Parmesan cheese

Brown the beef in a skillet, drain and mix with catsup, oregano, and basil in a mixing bowl and set aside. Prepare dough from the hot roll mix, using the water and egg. Allow the dough to rest five minutes; divide the dough into 16 to 20 pieces, press or roll each piece to form about a 4-inch diameter flat piece of dough. Stuff some of the beef mixture and grated cheese in the center of each flat dough, wrap the dough completely around the stuffing and place the sealed dough-side down in an oiled baking pan. Allow the stuffed rolls to rise in a closed, warm area for about 30 minutes.

When the rolls have risen, brush the tops with melted margarine and sprinkle Parmesan cheese on the tops. Bake about 20 minutes, making certain the rolls in the center of the pan are done. Makes 16–20 rolls.

SCONES

2 cups flour	1 cup cheese, grated
1 tbsp baking powder	2 eggs
1/4 tsp salt	2/3 cup milk
1 tbsp margarine	

Mix flour, baking powder, and salt. Cut in margarine with a fork, then stir in cheese. In a small bowl beat eggs, then add milk, stir and pour into dry ingredients. Stir the mixture and place on a well floured bread board. Roll or pat the dough to a thickness of about 1/2 inch, cut the dough in small squares or 1-inch wide strips; or you can roll dough balls about 1 inch in diameter and press these into round shapes about 1/2 inch thick. Place the cut out dough in an oiled baking pan and bake about 15 minutes. Can serve 8.

BASIC BANNOCK BREAD

1 cup flour	1/4 tsp salt
1 tsp baking powder	water

Mix ingredients with a few tablespoons of water. Bake 20–30 minutes in covered oven. The dough can bake as large loaf or several small ones. Serves 4.

Variations
1. Using milk instead of water adds flavor and makes a browner loaf.
2. 1 tbsp sugar adds flavor.
3. One egg makes bread richer.
4. 1 tbsp margarine makes bread flakier.
5. Add cinnamon or flavorings as desired.

TOAST

margarine   bread

Melt margarine on griddle, skillet or open Dutch oven. Place pieces of bread on the oiled surface, turning when brown on one side. Continue adding margarine as more bread is toasted.

MUFFINS

1¾ cups flour   1 egg, beaten
3 tbsp sugar   1 cup milk
1 tbsp baking powder   6 tbsp cooking oil
¾ tsp salt

Place flour, sugar, baking powder, and salt in a bowl. Add egg, milk and cooking oil to the bowl and stir until the batter is smooth.

Place cupcake papers in a muffin pan or cupcake holders. If cupcake papers are not used, oil each muffin cup holder. Fill cupcake papers or muffin cup about ⅔ full of batter.

Bake 20–25 minutes in covered oven. Serves 8.

Variations
1. Add ½ cup raisins or fresh fruit to batter.
2. Add cinnamon or nutmeg to batter.
3. Add vanilla, almond, or lemon flavoring.

BACON-CHEESE MUFFINS

For each person to be served:
2 slices bacon   2 oz cheese, grated
1 English muffin, sliced   parsley flakes or dill
2 tbsp margarine   weed

Cook the bacon until crisp and crumble bacon, setting aside.

Spread some margarine on each side of each half of the sliced muffins. On the top side of each half muffin, place the crumbled bacon and the grated cheese. Sprinkle some parsley flakes or dill weed on top of the cheese, place the muffin halves in a baking pan for oven heating or directly in the bottom of a Dutch oven. If an oven is not available, the muffins can be heated in a covered, heavy skillet. Heat for about five minutes or until the cheese is bubbly.

CRAB MEAT MUFFIN

For each person to be served:

1 English muffin, sliced	2 oz cream cheese
2 tbsp margarine	parsley flakes
2 oz crab meat, drained	

Spread some margarine on each side of each half of the sliced muffin. On the top side of each half muffin place the crab meat and then spread on the cream cheese. Sprinkle a few parsley flakes on top of the cheese, place the muffin halves in a baking pan for oven heating or directly in the bottom of a Dutch oven. If an oven is not available, the muffins can be heated in a covered, heavy skillet. Heat for about five minutes or until the cheese is warm and soft.

DUMPLINGS

biscuit mix   flour

Prepare biscuit dough mixture from either a dry biscuit mix or from basic ingredients. Roll on floured surface or pat by hand and form biscuits of 1 to 1½ -inch diameter. Place these biscuits on top of meat that is stewing in the oven. Cover and cook about 30 minutes.

You may want to spoon the dough into small balls and drop them into the stew.

WHOLE WHEAT HOT CAKES

7/8 cup whole wheat   2 tbsp cooking oil
     flour   1 egg
1 tbsp sugar   1/2 cup milk
1/4 tsp salt   1 tbsp bran, optional
1 tbsp baking powder

Mix the flour, baking powder, sugar and salt in a mixing bowl. Add oil, egg and milk, stir well.

Pour batter in small amounts on a hot griddle. Allow the cakes to bubble well and turn each cake one time. When cooked on the other side, remove the cakes to a warm container or directly onto warmed individual plates.

If the batter becomes too thick, add a tbsp of water, stir to thin batter. The above ingredients will make from 10 to 15 hot cakes, depending on your size of batter poured for each. You may increase your batter mix in these proportions to serve more people.

Desserts

BANANA PUDDING

6 oz vanilla wafers	2 tsp flour
3 bananas	1 egg, beaten
½ cup sugar	1 cup milk
4 tbsp margarine, melted	½ tsp vanilla extract

Place a layer of vanilla wafers in the bottom of an 8-inch square pan, slice bananas on top of the wafers. Combine the other ingredients, cooking in a sauce pan until thick. Pour over the bananas and then place vanilla wafers on the top. This can be prepared ahead and served cool. Serves 4–6.

OVEN BANANA PUDDING

For a simple pudding that can be prepared and cooked in your oven, try this one. Serve while warm.

6 oz vanilla wafers	1 egg, beaten
3 bananas	1 cup milk
½ cup sugar	½ tsp lemon flavoring
4 tbsp margarine	

Oil an 9-inch square baking pan and place vanilla wafers on the bottom of the pan. Slice two bananas into the pan and sprinkle one half the sugar over them. Slice the other banana and sprinkle the other half of the sugar on top. Place the margarine on top of the sugar.

In a bowl mix the egg, milk and flavoring, pour into the baking pan. Cook 30 minutes, remove from the oven and place an additional layer of vanilla wafers on top. Serves 8.

BANANA PUDDING

6 oz vanilla wafers
3 bananas

1 3-$\frac{1}{8}$-oz package vanilla
    pudding mix
1 egg, beaten

Place a layer of vanilla wafers in the bottom of an 8-inch square pan, slice bananas on top of the wafers. Cook the pudding mix as directed on the package with the egg added and pour over the bananas. Place more vanilla waters on the top. This can be prepared ahead and served cool. Serves 4 to 6.

BREAD PUDDING

$\frac{1}{2}$ cup margarine
1$\frac{1}{2}$ cups milk
1 cup sugar
4 cups day-old bread
    cubes

$\frac{1}{2}$ cup raisins
$\frac{1}{2}$ tsp nutmeg
$\frac{1}{8}$ tsp salt
3 eggs
cinnamon

Melt margarine in pan, add milk and heat. Add sugar and stir until sugar dissolves. Add bread cubes, raisins, nutmeg, and salt. Beat eggs and stir in mixture. Pour into an oiled baking pan, then sprinkle cinnamon on top.

Place baking pan in oven and bake 40–50 minutes.

When done, serve on plates and add dessert sauce (page 124), if desired. Serves 8.

Variations
1. Use brown sugar on top rather than cinnamon.
2. Use yogurt rather than a sauce.

CHOCOLATE PUDDING

½ cup sugar
2 tbsp cornstarch
2 tbsp cocoa
1 tbsp margarine

2 cups milk
1 tsp almond extract
chocolate chips or
    miniature marshmallows

Place sugar, cornstarch, and cocoa in sauce pan, mix well. Add margarine and milk and cook over low fire until the pudding is thick. Add extract and stir well. Pour pudding in cups or serving dishes. Serves 4.

Variations
    1. Place a few miniature marshmallows in each serving dish and pour the pudding in each dish.
    2. After pouring pudding in serving dishes, drop four or five chocolate chips on top of each serving.

CHOCOLATE PUDDING

1 3-½-oz chocolate
    pudding mix

¼ cup chocolate chips
2 cups milk

Prepare pudding mix by directions on package with milk and cook in a sauce pan. When the pudding is done, remove from the fire, stir the chocolate chips in the pudding and pour into four serving cups. The pudding can be served warm or cool. Serves 4.

CHERRY PUDDING

½ cup margarine,
    melted
2 tbsp sugar
2 cups graham crackers,
    crushed
1 tsp almond flavoring

2 3-⅛ -oz packages of
    vanilla pudding mix
4 cups milk
1 16-oz can sweet
    cherries, pitted

Melt margarine and combine with sugar and graham cracker crumbs. Line the bottom of an oiled 9-inch square pan. Prepare pudding mix with milk, as directed on package. Mix drained cherries and flavoring in pudding batter and pour into the pan. Cool for serving. Serves 8.

TAPIOCA PUDDING

3 tbsp tapioca	1 egg, beaten
½ cup sugar	2 cups milk
⅛ tsp salt	½ tsp lemon extract

Mix tapioca, sugar, salt, and egg in the milk, let stand 10 minutes. Bring the mixture to a boil, stirring continuously. Remove from the fire and stir in extract. Pour in individual serving cups and let it stand. The pudding can be served warm or later when cool. Garnish the top of each dessert container with a cherry or chunk of pineapple, if desired. Serves 4.

Variation
You can use almond or maple flavoring instead of lemon extract.

TAPIOCA PUDDING

2 3-oz Tapioca pudding mix	½ tsp lemon extract
	1 egg beaten

Place pudding mix in mixing bowl, as instructed on the pudding mix package. Add egg and mix well. Cook the pudding, as directed, remove from the fire and stir in extract, and pour into cup cake papers, in a dessert mold or serving dish. Can be served warm or cool. Garnish the top of each dessert mold with a cherry or chunk of pineapple, if desired. Serves 4.

Variation
You can use almond or maple flavoring instead of lemon extract.

BUTTERMILK PUDDING

1¼ cups sugar
3 tbsp flour
½ tsp ground nutmeg
3 eggs, beaten

1 cup buttermilk
¼ cup margarine, melted
1 tsp lemon extract

Mix sugar, flour, and nutmeg. Add eggs, buttermilk and margarine, stir well. Add extract and stir.

Pour into oiled baking pan and bake for about 45 minutes. If you have adequate oven space, you could pour this batter in eight oiled custard dishes and bake about 35 minutes. Serves 8.

FRUIT PUDDING

3 tbsp tapioca
½ cup sugar
⅛ tsp salt
1 egg, beaten

2½ cups milk
1 tsp almond flavoring
1 16-oz can blueberries,
    drained

Put tapioca, sugar, salt, egg, and milk in a sauce pan and let it set for 10 minutes. Bring the mixture to a boil, stirring constantly. Remove from the heat, add flavoring and fruit, stir and let it set for 20 minutes, then pour into 8 pudding cups. Serve warm or cool. Serves 8.

VINEGAR PUDDING

1¼ cups sugar
2 tbsp cornstarch
2 eggs, beaten

3 tbsp vinegar
1 tsp almond extract
1½ cups water

Mix sugar and cornstarch in a bowl. Add eggs and mix well. Add vinegar, extract and water, stir. Place in a sauce pan and cook over slow heat until thick. Pour the pudding into eight muffin cups lined with cupcake papers. Serve warm or cool. Serves 8.

CRANBERRY PUDDING

This uses the vinegar pudding recipe and substitutes cranberry cocktail juice for the 1½ cups water. This provides a flavorful pink pudding.

1¼ cups sugar
2 tbsp cornstarch
2 eggs, beaten
3 tbsp vinegar

1 tsp almond extract
1½ cups cranberry cocktail juice

Mix sugar and cornstarch in a bowl. Add eggs and mix well. Add vinegar, extract and juice, stir. Place in a sauce pan and cook over slow heat until thick. Pour the pudding into eight muffin cups lined with cupcake papers. Serve warm or cool. Serves 8.

EGG CUSTARD PUDDING

3 eggs
1 12-oz can of condensed
    milk
½ cup sugar

4 tbsp flour
3 tbsp margarine, melted
nutmeg

Beat eggs, add milk and sugar. In a separate cup, stir flour and margarine until smooth, then add to milk mixture. Stir mixture well and pour into eight muffin cups. Bake in an oven for about 45 minutes. Sprinkle nutmeg on top of pudding cups when removed from the oven. Serves 8.

VANILLA PUDDING

1 3-⅛-oz vanilla
    pudding mix
2 cups milk

1 egg, beaten
½ tsp almond flavoring
ground nutmeg

Combine pudding mix and milk. Add egg and cook as directed on the package. When it is cooked, add flavoring, stir and pour into serving cups. Sprinkle some nutmeg on top of each serving. The pudding can be served warm or cool. Serves 4.

Instead of the nutmeg, you may use ground cinnamon or brown sugar.

PAN COBBLER

2 tbsp margarine, melted
¾ cup sugar
1 cup whole wheat flour
1 tbsp baking powder

1 cup milk
1 21-oz can of pie
    filling

Combine margarine, sugar, flour, baking powder, and milk in a mixing bowl, stir well. Place batter in an oiled baking pan, add the pie filling over the whole of the batter. Bake about 45 minutes. Serves 8.

EASY COBBLER

1 large can sliced peaches
1 pkg yellow cake mix

margarine
cinnamon

Pour entire can of peaches and juice into an oiled baking pan. Then add the dry cake mix on top of the peaches. Place several pieces of margarine on top, and sprinkle cinnamon over all. Place in the oven and bake about 45 minutes, or until done. Serves 8.

Variations

1. Stir the cake mix and peaches when placed in the pan to provide a more spongy layer cake.

2. Use canned apples instead of peaches, and add 1 tsp cinnamon and 1 tsp allspice to the apples.

3. Use canned cherries instead of peaches, and add more sugar with the cherries.

APPLE CRUMB CAKE

2 cups flour
½ cup sugar
½ tsp salt
1 pkg yeast
½ cup milk, warmed
½ cup butter
2 eggs

2 large tart apples,
  sliced
⅔ cup brown sugar
½ cup flour
1 tbsp cinnamon
6 tbsp butter

In a bowl, mix 1 cup of the flour, sugar, salt, and yeast. Add warmed milk and mix well. Add butter, eggs and the other 1 cup flour and mix well. Pour batter into greased pan; place sliced apples on top of batter.

Combine brown sugar, flour, cinnamon, and butter in separate bowl. Mix until crumbly. Sprinkle this crumbly mix over apples and set pan aside in a warm place for 1 hour.

Bake about 30–40 minutes. Serves 8.

APPLESAUCE CAKE

1 cup margarine
2 cups brown sugar
1 16-oz can applesauce
3 cups flour

2 tsp baking soda
½ tsp salt
2 tsp cinnamon

Cream margarine and sugar (this means to blend the margarine and sugar into a thick creamy mixture); mix in applesauce. Combine flour, soda, salt, and cinnamon, and stir into the mixture.

Place in oiled baking pan and bake for 50–60 minutes. Serves 8–10.

BANANA-BAR LOAF

3 cups biscuit mix
¾ cup sugar
1 egg, beaten
¾ cup water

6 oz Heath bar chips or
    favorite candy bar
1 cup mashed bananas

Combine biscuit mix, sugar, egg and water, stir well. Add crushed candy bar and bananas and mix. Pour into an oiled cake pan and bake for 40–45 minutes. Serves 8.

BANANA LOAF

½ cup margarine
½ cup brown sugar
2 eggs, beaten
1 cup whole wheat flour
1 cup quick oats

½ tsp salt
1 tsp baking soda
2 cups mashed bananas
¼ cup milk

In a bowl blend the margarine and sugar; then add the beaten eggs. In another bowl mix flour, oats, salt, and soda; then add this to blended mixture. Add bananas and milk; then stir well. Pour batter into an oiled Pan and bake it in the oven for about 50-60 minutes. Turn out of pan onto serving plate. Serves 8.

Variation

Add chopped pecans to batter, or place pecan pieces in baking pan before pouring the batter in the pan.

QUICK CINNAMON ROLLS

3 cups biscuit mix flour
3–4 oz raisins

1 cup brown sugar
cinnamon

Mix the biscuit mix as directed and pat out in a rectangular shape on a floured, flat surface. Spread raisins and brown sugar over the dough. Sprinkle with cinnamon. Beginning with one long side of the dough, with floured hands, roll the dough into a cylinder. Cut slices from this rolled cylinder and place in an oiled baking pan. Place pan in an oven and bake about 15–20 minutes. Serves 8.

GINGERBREAD

½ cup margarine	1 tsp soda
1 cup brown sugar	½ tsp salt
1 egg	½ tsp ginger
½ cup molasses	1 tsp cinnamon
½ cup hot water	½ tsp allspice
1½ cups flour	¼ tsp cloves

Cream margarine, sugar, and egg. Blend in molasses and water. Add other dry ingredients and stir to mix dough. Put in greased pan and place in the oven and bake about 30–40 minutes, testing for doneness. Serves 8.

MINCEMEAT LOAF

2 cups flour	2 eggs
1 cup sugar	¼ cup margarine, melted
1 tbsp baking powder	1 tsp vanilla
½ tsp salt	9 oz mincemeat

Mix flour, sugar, baking powder, and salt in a bowl. In separate bowl beat eggs, add melted margarine and vanilla; mix with dry ingredients. Stir in mincemeat, prepared as directed on package. Pour batter into an oiled baking pan.

Bake one hour or until batter is done through the center. Cool 15 minutes and remove from container. Serves 8.

Variations

1. Add ½ cup chopped pecans to the batter.

2. In a small bowl, mix 1 cup confectioner's sugar and a small amount of milk; stir to smooth glaze. Pour glaze on cake top after it is removed from the pan.

3. Sprinkle confectioner's sugar on cake after it is removed from oven.

CHEESECAKE

1 cup Graham cracker crumbs	3 tbsp sugar
4 tsp margarine, melted	2 eggs, beaten
1 cup cottage cheese	nutmeg
8 oz. cream cheese	

Mix Graham cracker crumbs and margarine, line the bottom of an oiled 9-inch baking pan. Mix and beat the cottage cheese, cream cheese, sugar and eggs; pour this on the crust and sprinkle nutmeg on top. Bake about 45 minutes, then remove it to cool. Serves 8.

You may pour some fruit topping on servings.

NON COOK CHEESE CAKE

2 cups Graham crackers	½ cup hot water
2 tbsp sugar	1 cup cottage cheese
½ cup margarine, melted	¼ cup warm water
½ cup margarine, warmed	1 tbsp gelatin
1 cup sugar	juice of 2 lemons
½ cup dry milk	1 20-oz can of cherry pie filling

For crust, crumble Graham crackers, add sugar and mix with the ½ cup melted margarine. Press the graham cracker mix on bottom of oiled 8-inch square pan.

Combine warmed margarine, sugar, dry milk and hot water. Mix well and stir in cottage cheese. Stir warm water and gelatin in a cup, adding lemon juice; add to combined mix. Stir entire mix and pour onto crust in pan. Chill for an hour or two.

Add can of cherry pie filling to top of cheese cake. Chill until needed. Serves 8.

You can prepare this the day before and have it available to carry in your ice box cooler. You may wish to substitute blueberry filling for the fruit topping.

HILL COUNTRY COFFEE CAKE

2¼ cups flour	¾ cup cooking oil
½ tsp salt	1 tsp soda
1 tbsp cinnamon	1 tsp baking powder
1 cup brown sugar	1 egg, beaten
¾ cup sugar	1 cup buttermilk

Mix ingredients well and place in an oiled baking pan in oven. Bake 30 minutes, test for doneness. Serves 8.

Variations

1. Sprinkle ½ cup chopped pecans on top after batter is in baking pan.

2. Pour mixture of confectioners sugar and milk on top after cooking and removing from oven.

3. Add 1 tsp lemon flavoring to batter.

4. Sprinkle brown sugar on top after batter is in baking pan.

CREAM CHEESE CAKE

6 oz margarine	3 eggs, beaten
4 oz cream cheese	1½ cups flour
1½ cups sugar	½ tsp lemon extract

Cream margarine, cream cheese, and sugar well. Add eggs and flour, stir well. Add extract and stir.

Pour into an oiled baking pan and bake for about 60–70 minutes, test to be sure the cake is done.

This cake will usually do better in a tube-type pan. Place a small metal can in the center of your baking pan to allow a well of heat. Serves 6–8.

PEPPERMINT CAKE

1 cup margarine
2 cups sugar
4 eggs
2 tsp peppermint extract
1 tsp butter flavoring

½ tsp salt
3 cups flour
¾ cup buttermilk
½ cup peppermint candy,
   crushed

Cream margarine and sugar. Add eggs and beat well. Mix in extract, flavoring, and salt. Add flour and buttermilk in small amounts, stirring well. When batter is thoroughly mixed, add crushed candy and stir throughout gently.

Pour into tube pan and bake for about 1 hour. Test for doneness with straw. Serves 8.

POPPY SEED CAKE

1 cup whole wheat flour
1 cup white flour
1 cup sugar
½ tsp salt
2 tsp baking powder
2 tbsp poppy seed

¼ cup margarine, melted
1 egg, beaten
1 cup milk
4 tbsp margarine
4 tbsp brown sugar

Combine flours, sugar, salt, baking powder, and poppy seed. Add margarine, egg, and milk, stir well. Pour batter in an oiled baking pan and bake for 10 minutes. Remove pan and sprinkle small pieces of margarine and the brown sugar on top of the batter. Continue baking the cake batter an additional 30 minutes or until done. Serves 8 to 10.

SOUR CREAM CAKE

1 cup margarine
3 cups sugar
4 eggs
1 tsp vanilla extract
1 tsp almond extract

½ tsp salt
½ tsp soda
3 cups flour
1 cup sour cream

Cream margarine and sugar. Add eggs and beat well. Mix in extracts, salt, and soda. Add flour and sour cream in small amounts, stirring well. Place in oiled tube pan and bake for 50–60 minutes. Serves 8–10.

Variation

Sprinkle confectioner's sugar on cake after removing it from oven.

MARSHMALLOW TOP CAKE

2 cups biscuit mix	1 tsp vanilla
1/2 cup brown sugar	1 1/2 cups small marshmallows
1 egg, beaten	1/2 cup brown sugar
1/2 cup water	
2 tbsp margarine, melted	

Mix biscuit mix, sugar, egg, water, margarine, and vanilla. Pour into oiled cake pan. Bake 15 minutes in oven. Add marshmallows on top of batter and sprinkle the additional sugar on top. Bake about 10 minutes more. Serves 6 to 8.

PINEAPPLE UPSIDE-DOWN CAKE

1/4 cup margarine	1 yellow cake mix
1/2 cup brown sugar	1 egg
1 can sliced pineapple	

Place margarine and brown sugar in a pan and stir until well mixed. Place the pineapple slices in the butter and sugar mixture in a baking pan.

In a separate bowl, mix the cake mix and the egg. Pour this batter over the pineapple and bake about 30 to 40 minutes. Test the cake for doneness with a straw.

When the cake is done, remove the pan from the oven. Using a large cutting board or a piece of corrugated cardboard covered with waxed paper, hold the board on top of the pan and invert the pan quickly. This will allow the cake to fall on the board and the pineapple will be on the top.

Variations

1. Cherries may be placed in the pineapple to provide color.
2. Crushed pineapple may be used for a more uniform topping.

SHORTBREAD BARS

½ cup margarine, melted	¼ tsp salt
⅓ cup sugar	1¼ cups flour

Combine margarine, sugar, and salt, mix well. Add flour, mix thoroughly and pat or roll on a heavily floured surface. Cut dough into small square or rectangular shaped bars. Place bars on an oiled baking pan and bake about 15 minutes. Makes 24 to 30 bars.

An alternate way to shape these cookies is to pinch off small pieces of dough and roll into balls about 1 inch in diameter. Then place the balls on the baking pan and flatten the dough balls with your fingers or floured fork.

The shortbread is satisfactory plain, but you may wish to sprinkle a decorative topping of confectioners sugar or a cinnamon/sugar mixture. Another good variation is to press a pecan half on top of the shortbread before baking.

SURPRISE MUFFINS

Filling:

1 3-oz package of cream cheese	2 tbsp cocoa
	4 tbsp sugar

For a surprise filling, mix the warm cream cheese, sugar and cocoa in a bowl. Set aside.

Prepare the regular muffin batter (page 131) and fill the muffin pans about one-third full. Drop a spoonful of filling in the middle of each muffin pan of batter and add additional batter to fill about two- thirds of each muffin pan. Bake about 20 minutes. Serves 8.

CHOCOLATE CHIP BARS

½ cup margarine, melted	1 cup Graham cracker crumbs
½ cup brown sugar	6 oz chocolate chips
½ cup whole wheat flour	1 cup small marshmallows

Mix margarine, sugar, flour, and crumbs, then press the mixture in the bottom of an oiled 9-inch cake pan. Pour chips evenly on the crust and then pour the marshmallows on top. Bake about 15 minutes. Remove the pan and allow it to cool, then cut into bars. Serves 8.

BUTTER BARS

2 sticks butter	2 cups flour
1 lb brown sugar	2 tsp baking powder
1 cup sugar	1/2 tsp salt
4 eggs	1 tsp vanilla

Blend butter and sugar, add eggs and beat. Add other dry ingredients and stir until well mixed. Pour into an oiled baking pan and place in the oven.

Cook 30–40 minutes and remove from oven. Allow the pan to cool for 10 minutes, cut in rectangular bars and serve warm.

CHOCOLATE CUPS

3/4 cup margarine, melted	4 tbsp sugar
1 cup Graham cracker crumbs	6 oz chocolate chips
	1 cup small marshmallows
	1/2 cup whole wheat flour

Mix margarine, Graham cracker crumbs, flour, and sugar. Divide mix into equal portions and press on the bottom and partially up the sides of eight oiled muffin cups. Place the chocolate chips in the molded crusts, then place the marshmallows on top. Place in the oven and bake 15 minutes. Cool and serve in the muffin pans. Serves 8.

FUDGE SQUARES

¾ cup margarine
½ cup cocoa
¾ cup flour
1½ cups sugar

1 tsp vanilla
3 eggs, beaten
½ cup chopped pecans

Heat margarine and cocoa until margarine melts, set aside.

Mix flour and sugar in a bowl; add vanilla and the beaten eggs. Add margarine and cocoa ingredients to the mixture; stir in pecans. Pour batter into an oiled baking pan.

Bake for 40–50 minutes. Remove cake to cool about 15 minutes and cut into squares. Serves 8.

ANISE COOKIES

¼ cup margarine,
   softened
¾ cup sugar
2 eggs, beaten

½ tsp anise seed
1½ cups flour
pecan halves or slivered
   almonds

Cream margarine and sugar, stir in eggs. Stir in anise seed and gradually mix in flour. Pinch off small amounts of dough and roll between the palms of your hands into balls about 1 inch in diameter. Place these balls of dough in your oiled baking pan and press to a thickness of about ¼ inch. Place a pecan half or slivered almond piece on top of each cookie.

Bake about 25 minutes. Remove cookies from pan. Makes about 24 to 30 cookies.

COCOA-CHIP COOKIES

½ cup margarine
1 cup sugar
1 egg, beaten
1 tsp almond extract
1¾ cups flour

6 tbsp cocoa
½ tsp baking soda
¼ tsp salt
¾ cup buttermilk
¾ cup chocolate chips

Mix margarine, sugar, egg, and extract together. In a separate bowl combine flour, cocoa, soda and salt. Combine and mix these dry ingredients, add to the main batter and then add the buttermilk and mix well. Add chocolate chips and stir the batter. Drop spoonfuls of the batter on an oiled baking pan and bake about 10 minutes. Remove the cookies to cool on a flat surface. Makes 40–50 cookies.

PRALINE CRACKERS

1 cup margarine, melted	1 cup pecans, finely
1 cup brown sugar	chopped
	Graham crackers

Melt margarine, add sugar and, while stirring, bring to a boil for one minute. Stir in pecans. This mixture will be the topping.

Arrange graham crackers in one layer in an oiled baking pan. Pour enough topping to slightly cover the Graham crackers. Bake 10 to 12 minutes in your oven, cool the pan for a few minutes. Remove the crackers with a spatula and place them on waxed paper for serving.

Additional crackers can be placed in the oiled pan, covered with some of the remaining topping and then baked as above. Repeat as needed.

PECAN DROPS

1 cup margarine	2 tsp vanilla
1/3 cup sugar	2 cups flour
2 tsp water	1 cup pecans, chopped

Blend margarine and sugar. Add water and vanilla and mix well. Add flour and pecans and stir to a smooth batter. Drop spoonfuls of batter on a greased pan and place pan in the oven.

Bake about 15 minutes. Makes about 50 cookies.

OATMEAL COOKIES

$\frac{1}{2}$ cup margarine $\frac{1}{2}$ tsp salt
$\frac{3}{4}$ cup brown sugar   1 tsp baking powder
1 egg $\frac{1}{2}$ tsp cinnamon
$\frac{1}{4}$ cup milk $\frac{1}{2}$ tsp nutmeg
1 cup flour $1\frac{1}{2}$ cups quick oats

Blend margarine sugar, and egg; then mix in milk. Add the dry ingredients and oats and stir to a smooth mixture. Drop spoonfuls of batter on a oiled pan and place the pan in the oven.

Bake about 15 minutes. Makes about 40 cookies.

Variation
Add $\frac{1}{2}$ cup raisins

PEANUT BUTTER COOKIES

$\frac{1}{2}$ cup peanut butter $\frac{1}{2}$ tsp vanilla
$\frac{1}{2}$ cup margarine $1\frac{1}{4}$ cups flour
1 cup sugar $\frac{1}{2}$ tsp baking powder
1 cup brown sugar $\frac{1}{2}$ tsp soda
1 egg, beaten $\frac{1}{4}$ tsp salt

Cream peanut butter, margarine, and sugars. Then mix in egg and vanilla. Add the flour mixed with baking powder, soda, and salt. Mix well and form the dough into balls about 1 inch in diameter. Place these on an oiled pan; flatten the dough balls with a floured fork.

Bake about 15 minutes. Will make about 40 cookies.

PEANUT BUTTER NUGGETS

1 cup peanut butter   1 egg, beaten
1 cup sugar   1 tsp vanilla

Put ingredients in a bowl and mix well. Form the dough into balls about 1 inch in diameter. Place these on an oiled pan. Flatten the dough balls with a floured fork.

Bake about 15 minutes. Will make about 40 cookies.

PECAN BALLS

¼ lb margarine,
  softened
¾ cup confectioner's
  sugar

½ cup pecans, chopped
1 cup flour

Cream margarine and sugar. Stir in pecans and then gradually mix in flour. Pinch off small amounts of dough and roll between the palms of your hands into balls about 1 inch in diameter. Place these balls of dough in your oiled baking pan and press to a thickness of about ½ inch.
Bake about 20 minutes. Makes about 20 cookies.

SUGAR COOKIES

⅔ cup margarine
¾ cup sugar
1 tsp lemon flavoring
½ tsp vanilla flavoring
1 egg

4 tsp milk
2 cups flour
1½ tsp baking powder
¼ tsp salt

Blend margarine, sugar, and flavorings. Add egg and beat. Mix in milk and dry ingredients and stir well. Roll dough on floured surface and cut with biscuit cutter. Place cookies in a greased pan and bake in an oven about 15 minutes. Makes about 40 cookies.

Variations
Instead of lemon flavoring, use one of these:
1. 1 tsp ginger and 1 tsp cinnamon
2. 1 tsp almond flavoring
3. 1 tsp anise seeds

BISCUIT MIX COOKIES

¾ cup biscuit mix   1 egg, beaten
1 3½-oz pudding mix   ¼ cup margarine, melted

Combine biscuit mix, pudding mix, egg and margarine and stir well. Using your hands, form dough into small balls, place the balls on an oiled cookie pan and flatten the dough balls to about ¼-inch thickness. This makes about 20 cookies. Bake 10 minutes.

Variations
1. Use chocolate pudding mix and add ¼ cup chocolate chips.
2. Use butterscotch pudding mix and add ¼ cup butterscotch morsels or chopped pecans.

MOLASSES SQUARES

6 tbsp margarine, melted   ½ cup powdered sugar
⅓ cup molasses   ½ cup whole wheat flour
1 egg, beaten   ½ cup white flour
¼ tsp baking soda   1 tsp almond flavoring
⅛ tsp salt   powdered sugar

Mix margarine, molasses, egg, soda, and salt. Stir and add sugar. Stir in flour and flavoring. Place in oiled pan and bake 15 to 20 minutes. Remove and cool 10 minutes. Sprinkle powdered sugar on top and cut into squares. Makes 20–24 squares.

For molasses you may use ribbon cane, sorghum or dark corn syrup.

BOILED COOKIES

2 cups sugar   3 cups oatmeal, chopped
½ cup milk   ½ cup pecans, chopped
4 tbsp margarine   1 tsp vanilla
2 tbsp cocoa

Place sugar, milk, margarine, and cocoa in pan and bring to a boil, cook for 2 minutes. Remove pan from the fire and add the remaining ingredients. Stir well and then drop mixture from a spoon onto waxed paper, allowing cookies to cool. Makes 30 to 40 cookies.

PIE CRUST

2 cups flour	$2/3$ cup margarine
1 tsp salt	4–6 tbsp water

Blend, flour, salt, and margarine. Slowly mix in water, stirring with fork.

Divide dough, and on a floured surface pat or roll to needed size, allowing about 60% of the dough for the bottom crust. Place the bottom crust in a floured pan and then pour the fruit or other filling in the bottom crust.

The top crust or lattice strip dough can be patted or rolled on a floured surface, trimmed to desired size and placed on the top of the filling so that the edges of both crusts overlap. Dampen the edges of both crusts with a few drops of water and seal the two crusts together by pinching with the fingers or using a wet fork.

GRAHAM CRACKER CRUST

2 cups crushed Graham crackers crumbs	$1/2$ cup margarine, melted
	2 tbsp sugar

Mix ingredients well and press the mixture in the bottom of an oiled 9-inch round pan or 8-inch square pan.

PECAN PIES

Crust:

1 3-oz package cream cheese	1 cup flour
$1/2$ cup margarine	

Soften cream cheese and margarine, blend with flour. Divide dough into eight equal portions. Roll or pat out dough to fit cupcake pans. Press dough to bottoms and sides of cupcake pans.

Filling:

¾ cup brown sugar
1 tbsp flour
1 egg
1 tbsp milk

1 tsp vanilla
¼ cup margarine, melted
½ cup chopped pecans

Mix sugar and flour. Beat in egg, milk, vanilla, and margarine. Stir in chopped pecans. Pour mixture into the crust-lined pans.

Bake in oven 35–40 minutes. Remove pies and let them cool; then remove from pans. Serves 8.

CHESS PIE

½ cup brown sugar
1 cup sugar
1 tsp flour
2 eggs

1 tsp lemon flavoring
2 tbsp milk
½ cup margarine, melted
1 cup chopped pecans
(optional)

Mix sugars and flour. Beat in eggs, flavoring, milk, and margarine. Stir in pecans, if desired. Pour mixture into pie crust.

Bake in oven 40–45 minutes. Remove and let pie cool. Serves 8.

Variations

1. Instead of pecans, use 1 8-oz can of crushed pineapple, drained.
2. Instead of lemon flavoring, use vanilla.

CHESS CRUMB PIE

½ cup margarine, melted
3 tbsp sugar
2 cups Graham crackers, crushed
½ cup brown sugar
1 cup sugar

1 tbsp whole wheat flour
½ cup margarine, melted
2 eggs, beaten
1 tsp almond flavoring

Combine margarine, sugar, and Graham cracker crumbs. Press on the bottom and sides of an oiled 9-inch pie pan. Mix sugars, flour, margarine, eggs, and flavoring, then pour mixture into the crumb crust. Bake for 35 to 40 minutes and remove to cool for 20 minutes. Serves 6 to 8.

APPLE BUTTER

8 tart apples	1 cup sugar
1/4 cup water	2 tsp cinnamon

Peel and core apples, slice and place in a covered sauce pan. Add 1/4 cup water and cook on low heat for 20–30 minutes or until apples can be mashed with a slotted masher. Add cinnamon, mash and stir thoroughly. Serve warm. Serves 8.

You may want to add some allspice or nutmeg with the cinnamon. The apple butter can be served cold.

APPLE CUPS

4 cups tart apples, chopped	3/4 cup brown sugar
	1 tsp cinnamon
1/4 cup raisins	1 tbsp margarine, melted
2 tsp lemon juice	pie crust dough

Mix apples, raisins and lemon juice. Add sugar, cinnamon and margarine and stir well. Pour apple mixture in eight muffin cups.

Prepare a pie crust dough, roll it out and cut round pieces of dough to fit in top of each muffin cup. Bake in oven about 45 minutes or until crust is golden. Serves 8.

BRAISED BANANAS

2 tbsp margarine	1 tsp cinnamon
6 bananas	4 tbsp sugar

Melt margarine in skillet and place sliced bananas in skillet. Cook bananas about 4 or 5 minutes, turning the bananas to heat each side. Mix the cinnamon and sugar and sprinkle over the bananas. Serve warm. Serves 8.

PEAR COBBLER CUPS

1 29-oz can pear halves
1 4-oz jar maraschino
  cherries
½ tsp allspice
¾ cup biscuit mix

3 tbsp brown sugar
3 tbsp margarine, melted
½ cup fruit juice
  powdered sugar

Place cupcake papers in eight individual muffin cups. Drain and retain juice from the pears, placing a pear half in each cupcake paper. Drain and retain juice from cherries, placing a cherry in each pear half. Sprinkle allspice on pears.

Combine biscuit mix, sugar, margarine, and fruit juice to form a soft batter. Spoon the batter onto the fruit in the muffin cups. Bake about 20 minutes or until the top browns. Sprinkle powdered sugar on top, if desired. Serves 8.

You can use peach halves instead of pears.

POACHED PEARS

1 cup orange juice
¼ cup sugar

4 fresh pears

Combine juice and sugar in a large skillet and heat to boiling. Peel, quarter and core pears. Place pears in the juice, cover and cook about 15 minutes. Serve pears warm or cool. Serves 8.

Snacks

COTTAGE CHEESE DIP

2 cups cottage cheese   2 tsp dill weed
½ cup buttermilk

Blend or beat the cottage cheese to provide smaller particles. Add sufficient buttermilk to make the mix thin enough for the dip desired. Add dill weed and mix thoroughly.
The dip can be prepared ahead and left in refrigeration until needed.

SOUR CREAM DIP

1 cup sour cream   ⅛ tsp salt

Use this as a basic dip. For varieties use one of these:

2 tsp chopped chives
⅛ tsp onion salt
2 tsp horseradish
2 tsp dill weed
2 tsp dijon mustard
Prepare this dip ahead and let it age a few hours or overnight.

CREAM CHEESE DIP

2 8-oz packages of cream   ¼ tsp onion salt
   cheese   4 tbsp buttermilk
4 tbsp salad dressing

Combine cream cheese, salad dressing, and salt, mix well. This can be a basic dip. Thin with buttermilk, if needed.

Add a tsp dill weed for a tasty dip or add a tsp of horseradish for a spicy flavor.

MARINATED MUSHROOMS

For a before meal snack or complementary dish, marinate some mushrooms. If they are small you can leave them whole or slice the larger ones.

½ cup red vinegar   ½ tsp oregano
½ cup olive oil   ½ tsp dill weed
½ cup water   8 oz fresh mushrooms
½ tsp garlic salt

Combine the liquids and spices in a sauce pan and heat to almost boiling, simmer 5 to 10 minutes. Remove pan from fire and add mushrooms.

Place mushrooms and marinade sauce in a covered dish and allow them to set for several hours. Serve at open temperature. These can be refrigerated and used the next day. Serves 6 to 8.

CHEESE CRISPS

pie crust batch   Parmesan cheese
margarine

Prepare the pie crust recipe and roll dough to about ⅛-inch thickness. Cut the dough into small rounds with a biscuit cutter or use a knife to cut pieces about 1 inch by 2 inches. Brush margarine on the pieces and sprinkle cheese on top. Place the dough pieces in an oiled baking pan and bake for 12 to 15 minutes. Keep warm until served.

These can be served as a snack or with a meal. You can add flavor such as a pizza sauce instead of the margarine, or shake some dill weed on before the cheese.

PARCHED PEANUTS

Place 1–2 lb of unshelled peanuts in a pan in the oven. Bake about 30–40 minutes. During baking, occasionally stir peanuts to heat the whole batch evenly; test for doneness during the baking. Serve while warm.

TOASTED PECANS

margarine   salt
pecan halves

Melt a few tablespoons of margarine in a baking pan and add pecan halves. Rub some margarine on pecan halves; salt if desired.

Place the pan in an oven and bake for 15–20 minutes. Remove pecans and serve while warm.

Variations
1. Sprinkle pecans with sugar instead of salt.
2. Sprinkle cinnamon with the sugar.

POP CORN

margarine   salt
pop corn

Melt 4 oz of margarine in Dutch oven. Cover most of bottom of oven with one layer of pop corn. Place lid on oven and bake until the sounds indicate all the corn has popped. During the popping time, lift the oven by the bail and briskly rotate the oven to better stir the whole batch of corn. The corn can be popped in a heavy covered pan, shaking the pan often to stir the corn during cooking.

Pour popped corn into a paper bag, pour additional melted margarine and salt for desired taste. Shake the bag to distribute salt, serve while warm.

CARNIVAL APPLES

apples   raisins
sugar   cinnamon

Use tart apples such as Winesap, Jonathan, or Rome Beauty, if available. Cut cylindrical core from apples and place apples in a pan. In the core hole of each apple, place sugar, raisins, and cinnamon. Place pan in oven; cover and bake about 30 minutes.

S'MORES

Graham crackers   marshmallows
chocolate bars

Historically, these have been a simple well-liked camp dessert or snack. Basically they are made by taking a Graham cracker, placing a layer of chocolate candy on the cracker, then placing one or two semi-melted marshmallows on the chocolate, then another graham cracker on top. The warm, tasty combination usually calls for s'mores.

Various combinations of amounts or arrangement of the ingredients are preferred by some. Some cooks prefer to place the crackers and chocolate in an oven to warm while the marshmallows are toasting. Toast the marshmallows carefully to avoid overcooking or burning.

MULLED CIDER

2 qt cider   6 cloves
1 stick cinnamon

Place the cider in a covered pan to heat on low fire. Put the cinnamon and cloves in the cider and heat for an hour. You can cool the cider and reheat if needed. You can tie the cinnamon and cider in a cloth bag for easy removal.

HOT COCOA

A universal campfire or cook-out drink is hot cocoa. A convenient and good hot cocoa mix is available at grocery stores. The individual serving envelope of mix and hot water gives you a cup of hot cocoa.

If you do not have the prepared mix, you can prepare your own. To prepare the hot cocoa for four servings use:

⅓ cup cocoa	1 qt milk, heated
½ cup sugar	¾ tsp vanilla
⅛ tsp salt	
⅓ cup hot water	

In a sauce pan combine cocoa, sugar, salt and blend well with the hot water. Bring to a boil; stir constantly and boil for 2 minutes. Add heated milk, stir well and heat the mixture, do not boil. Remove from heat, add vanilla, stir vigorously and serve while hot.

You can also replace the need for carrying, refrigerating and heating the milk by using dry milk. Use 1⅓ cups of dry milk and a quart of hot water in the above mixture to serve four.

You can make an abbreviated mix for one cup by placing in your drinking cup:

1½ tbsp cocoa	1½ tbsp sugar
6 tbsp dry milk	

and adding hot water to your cup, stirring well.

SASSAFRAS TEA

Secure roots from the sassafras tree. You may uncover roots from a large tree and cut a few root sections or remove a whole small tree. I prefer roots of no larger than 1 inch in diameter, and I then cut the roots in pieces of about 1 inch in length. The larger diameter pieces can be split to allow more root exposure to the water.

After washing the root pieces, let them dry. For the root pieces to be retained for several weeks, you may wish to seal them in an air-tight container.

I prefer to brew the tea in a glass or enamel container to avoid any possible flavor change from a metal pan. If there is no other choice you can use a metal container.

Place about two quarts of water and three or four pieces of your sassafras root in the pot. Place the pot on a fire and let it simmer for an hour or so. The tea water should be a reddish color, the taste being a root beer type flavor. Some people like to add a little sugar to sweeten the tea. After you have served tea from the pot, you can add replacement water and brew additional tea from the same roots.

In past years, some claims have been made for the medicinal value of the tea, although I cannot verify this. The tea is enjoyed by many.

Index